Chris Roffey

Cambridge IGCSE® and O Level
Computer Science

Programming Book

For Python

CAMBRIDGE
UNIVERSITY PRESS

University Printing House, Cambridge CB2 8BS, United Kingdom

One Liberty Plaza, 20th Floor, New York, NY 10006, USA

477 Williamstown Road, Port Melbourne, VIC 3207, Australia

4843/24, 2nd Floor, Ansari Road, Daryaganj, Delhi – 110002, India

79 Anson Road, #06 -04/06, Singapore 079906

Cambridge University Press is part of the University of Cambridge.

It furthers the University's mission by disseminating knowledge in the pursuit of education, learning and research at the highest international levels of excellence.

Information on this title: www.cambridge.org

First published 2017

20 19 18 17 16 15 14 13 12 11 10 9 8 7 6 5 4 3

A catalogue record for this publication is available from the British Library

ISBN 978-1-316-61782-3 Paperback

Additional resources for this publication at www.cambridge.org

Cambridge University Press has no responsibility for the persistence or accuracy of URLs for external or third-party internet websites referred to in this publication, and does not guarantee that any content on such websites is, or will remain, accurate or appropriate. Information regarding prices, travel timetables, and other factual information given in this work is correct at the time of first printing but Cambridge University Press does not guarantee the accuracy of such information thereafter.

IGCSE is the registered trademark of Cambridge International Examinations

All examination-style questions, sample mark schemes, solutions and/or comments that appear in this book were written by the author. In examination, the way marks would be awarded to answers like these may be different.

....

Contents

Introduction   iv

How to use this book: a guided tour   vi

Acknowledgements   viii

1   Python 3   1

2   Sequence   8

3   Variables and Arithmetic Operators   14

4   Subroutines   23

5   GUI Applications (Optional)   30

6   Selection   37

7   Iteration   53

8   Designing Algorithms   72

9   Checking Inputs   81

10   Testing   92

11   Arrays   105

12   Pre-release Task Preparation   119

13   Examination Practice   128

14   Solutions   133

    Appendix – Tkinter Reference   193

Introduction

When Richard Morgan wrote the Visual Basic edition of this book he had two aims in mind. The first was to provide a programming book that specifically covered the material relevant to the Cambridge IGCSE® and O Level Computer Science syllabuses (0478/2210). The second, and perhaps more important, aim was to provide the student with a start to the exciting and rewarding process of being able to create their own computer programs. These are admirable aims that I hope have not been lost in this derivative translation into Python 3.

There are a few subtle changes to the flow diagrams and the pseudocode in this Python edition but fundamentally, wherever possible, the algorithms used are the same as those in the Visual Basic book. This has the exciting outcome that students can be taught the same material in a Cambridge IGCSE and O Level Computer Science class with a mixture of the two books. They can work on solutions in groups and then go and write the code for working implementations of their algorithms in either language.

Python and Visual Basic have different strengths and weaknesses and so they lend themselves to slightly different approaches. For this reason, the chapters have been slightly reordered in this book. The original Chapter 1 has been split: only text-based programming is introduced in Chapter 1 while how to produce GUIs has been moved to the optional Chapter 5. There is also an additional chapter on preparing for the pre-release task. All other chapter titles remain the same so easy comparison should be possible.

Language

The syntax and structures used to implement programming techniques will vary across different languages. This book is entirely based around Python 3, one of the three recommended languages for the Cambridge International AS and A Level syllabus. Python has, at its core, the principle that code should be easy to read. This means that in many ways it is very close to pseudocode.

The pseudocode structure used in the Cambridge IGCSE and O Level Computer Science examination papers uses a language neutral style. Although students are expected to be familiar with this and be able to read and follow the logic easily, they are not expected to produce their own pseudocode in exactly this style. Pseudocode is meant to be a way of expressing clearly the logic of a program, free from the worries of syntax.

Python also has a recommended style guide that can be found at https://www.python.org/dev/peps/pep-0008/.

Here, for example, it is recommended that Python programmers name functions and variables with descriptive all lower case characters separated by underscores, for example `my_variable`. This style is never used in Cambridge IGCSE and O Level Computer Science pseudocode; however, students should not be marked down for doing so in their own pseudocode. As it could be very confusing to keep swapping naming conventions, this book assumes that students are going to stick, wherever possible, to the correct Python style but be flexible enough thinkers to be able to read other pseudocode styles. It is recommended that when preparing for exams, students ensure they are aware of the exam board variable naming style. Chapter 13 in this book provides some examination style questions.

Examination focused

The Cambridge IGCSE and O Level Computer Science course will test computational thinking independent of any specific programming language. It will do this through the use of program design tools such as structure diagrams and flowcharts. It will also make use of pseudocode, a structured method for describing the logic of computer programs.

It is crucial that the student becomes familiar with these techniques. Throughout this book all the programming techniques are demonstrated in the non-language-specific format required, with the exception of variable and function naming. This will help to prepare the student to answer the types of question they will meet in their studies.

To support learning, many of the chapters include examination-style tasks. Chapter 14 has examples of appropriate code solutions that show how to turn logical ideas into actual programs. There is also a series of examination-style questions in Chapter 13, which has a sample mark scheme giving possible solutions and showing where the marks might be awarded.

Developing programming skills

One of the advantages of Python is that it provides a language that encourages the student to program solutions making use of the basic programming constructs: sequence, selection and iteration. Although the language does have access to many powerful pre-written code libraries, they are not generally used in this book.

Computational thinking is the ability to break down a problem into its constituent parts and to provide a logical and efficient coded solution. Experience shows that knowing how to think computationally relies much more on an understanding of the underlying programming concepts than on the ability to learn a few shortcut library routines.

This book is aimed at teaching those underlying skills which can be applied to the languages of the future. It is without doubt that programming languages will develop over the coming years but the ability to think computationally will remain a constant.

How to use this book: a guided tour

72

Chapter 8:
Designing Algorithms

Learning objectives

By the end of this chapter you will understand:

- that systems are made up of subsytems, which may in turn be made up of further subsytems
- how to apply top-down design and structure diagrams to simplify a complex system
- how to combine the constructs of sequence, selection and iteration to design complex systems
- how to produce effective and efficient solutions to complex tasks.

Cambridge IGCSE and O Level Programming Book

Learning objectives – are included at the beginning of each chapter and present the learning aims for the unit.

This is very similar to the Cambridge IGCSE and O Level Computer Science pseudocode format:

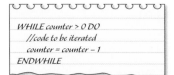

```
WHILE counter > 0 DO
    //code to be iterated
    counter = counter – 1
ENDWHILE
```

Key terms – provide clear definitions for the most important terms within each unit.

KEY TERMS

WHILE loop: A type of iteration that will repeat a sequence of code while a set of criteria continue to be met. If the criteria are not met at the outset the loop will not run and the code within it will not be executed.

SYLLABUS CHECK

Pseudocode: understand and use pseudocode, using WHILE . . . DO . . . ENDWHILE loop structures.

Syllabus checks – link programming concepts to points on the Cambridge IGCSE syllabus.

Each individual element of the loop performs an important role in achieving the iteration, as shown in Table 7.04.

62

Table 7.04

Element	Description
while	The start of the loop
counter > 0	The condition that controls the loop. Each time the iteration is run, the condition is evaluated and if it remains True, the iteration will run. Once the condition is False, execution of the code is directed to the line following the loop. In counter-controlled WHILE loops, it is important that code is included within the loop to increment or decrement the counter. In a FOR loop, the counter is automatically incremented. The same facility does not apply to WHILE loops and, as a result, the programmer must include appropriate code.
end of indented code	The end of the current iteration. Execution of the program returns to while so the condition can be re-evaluated and further iterations actioned. Do not forget to add ENDWHILE when writing pseudocode.

TIP

Remember that WHILE loops iterate while the condition evaluates to True. It is possible to create an infinite loop rather easily:

```
>>> while True:
        print('Hello', end='')
```

It is therefore important to know how to break out of infinite loops. To do so, hold down the _CTRL_ key on your keyboard and press _C_. Try the code above yourself in an interactive session. The optional parameter end='' provided in the print() function suppresses the default line return.

Tip boxes – offer quick suggestions to remind students about important learning points.

Task 2 – Discussion Question

a What is the aim of this flowchart?

b What kind of loop is being suggested here?

Extension tasks – build on task exercises to help the student further develop their knowledge and understanding.

Cambridge IGCSE and O Level Programming Book

11.07 Array Tasks

Task 6

a Draw a flowchart and create a pseudocode algorithm that iterates through an array of Integers and outputs the average. Declare and initialise the array with the following set of Integers: 12, 14, 10, 6, 7, 11 and 3.

b Test that your algorithm works by programming and running the code in Python.

Task 7

An algorithm will take an Integer value, n. It will call a subroutine to place into an array 12 incremental multiples of n (the first array index will hold $1 \times n$ and the last index position $12 \times n$). An additional subroutine will allow the user to output all the multiples in order.

a Draw a flowchart and create pseudocode for this algorithm.

b Test that your algorithm works by programming and running the code in Python.

Task 8

The data in Table 11.06 is to be organised in arrays so that the user can search via User ID and the system will display all the data related to that User ID.

Table 11.06

User ID	Age	Gender
112	45	Male
217	16	Female
126	27	Female

a Draw a flowchart and create a pseudocode algorithm that accepts a User ID and displays the related data.

b Test that your algorithm works by programming and running the code in Python.

Tasks – contain exercises for the student to test their knowledge of the topic.

Summary

- An array is a variable that can hold a set of data items, of the same data type, under a single identifier.

- When an array is declared, its size is defined. In Python indexes start from zero.

- Each element or data item in an array can be referenced by its index.

- The index can be used to read or write values in an array.

- A FOR loop can be used to iterate through the index locations in an array. The loop counter is used to identify successive index numbers.

- Holding records which consist of more than one data item can be achieved by the use of multiple arrays. Data for each record is held at the same index position in the different arrays.

- When using Python to implement algorithms involving arrays, a list is used as a substitute for an array.

Summary checklists – are included at the end of each chapter to review what the student has learned.

Acknowledgements

Thanks to the following for permission to reproduce images:

Cover image: Soulart/Shutterstock; Chapter opener 1 isak55/Shutterstock; Chapter opener 2 aimy27feb/Shutterstock; Chapter opener 3 Image Source/Getty Images;Chapter opener 4 Devrimb/iStock/Getty Images;Chapter opener 5 Andrew Brookes/Getty Images; Chapter opener 6 Magictorch/Ikon Images/Getty Images;Chapter opener 7 alexaldo/iStock/Getty Images;Chapter opener 8 Ioana Davies (Drutu)/Shutterstock; Chapter openers 9, 10 Kutay Tanir/Photodisc/Getty Images;Chapter opener 11 ILeysen/Shutterstock; Chapter opener 12 Kamil Krawczyk/E+/Getty Images; Chapter opener 13 Aeriform/Getty Images

Chapter 1:
Python 3

Learning objectives

By the end of this chapter you will understand how to:

- obtain a simple IDE to support your programming
- use both interactive mode and script mode in Python
- program and save a text-based application in script mode.

1.01 Getting Python 3 and IDLE For Your Computer

Python 3 is the latest version of the Python programming language. It is a loosely typed script language. Loosely typed means that it is usually not necessary to declare variable types; the interpreter looks after this. Script languages do not have a compiler. This means that, in general, Python programs cannot run as quickly as compiled languages; however, this brings numerous advantages, such as fast and agile development.

Python is a powerful, modern programming language used by many famous organisations such as YouTube and National Aeronautics and Space Administration (NASA) and it is one of the three programming languages that can be used to develop Google Apps.

There are installers for Windows and Apple computers available at https://www.python.org/downloads/. You should choose the latest stable version of Python 3 (Python 3.5.0 at time of writing). If you have a Raspberry Pi, then two versions of Python are already installed.

On the Raspberry Pi you can start programming in **interactive mode** straight away by selecting _Python 3_ from _Programming_ in the main _Menu_ in the task bar (Figure 1.01).

Figure 1.01 Starting Python 3 on a Raspberry Pi

This opens IDLE which is the **IDE** (Integrated Development Environment) that comes packaged with Python (Figure 1.02).

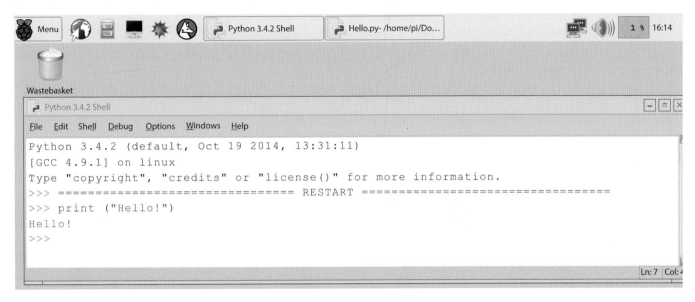

Figure 1.02 IDLE's Python Shell – working in interactive mode on a Raspberry Pi

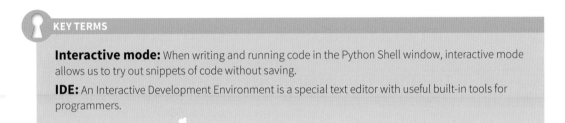

KEY TERMS

Interactive mode: When writing and running code in the Python Shell window, interactive mode allows us to try out snippets of code without saving.

IDE: An Interactive Development Environment is a special text editor with useful built-in tools for programmers.

After installing Python 3 on Apple computers, IDLE can be found in the main _Python 3_ folder in your _Applications_ folder.

On Windows computers, once installed, IDLE can be opened by looking for the _Python 3.5_ folder found in _All Programs_ when opening the _Start_ menu. From the _Python 3.5_ folder choose _IDLE_.

In all cases this opens a window containing the Python Shell. This can run simple programs at the >>> prompt. Executing small programs in the Shell window is referred to as working in interactive mode. It provides a very useful environment for running short code experiments when developing larger programs in **script mode**. Throughout this book you will be prompted to try out code snippets and run short experiments so that you get used to new functions and syntax in interactive sessions. These sessions can be accessed extremely quickly by opening IDLE and typing directly into the Shell window.

KEY TERMS

Script mode: When writing code in a new window in IDLE that will be saved in a file as a Python script.

To create a script that can contain more complex programs and, more significantly, can be saved and reused, you should obtain a new window by selecting _New File_ from the _File_ menu. This opens a blank script window into which you can type and save your code (always with the extension .py). IDLE provides help with code colouring and auto-indenting in whichever mode you are working.

In script mode, the Shell window takes on a new role as a console. Text output from your programs appears in this window (see Figure 1.03). It is also where users provide input, and error messages appear. The console is still available as a Shell window to use for quick experiments while developing your scripts.

To run your scripts, you should save your file to a sensibly named folder in your _Documents_ folder and then select _Run Module_ from the _Run_ menu, or press F5 on your keyboard.

Figure 1.03   IDLE's Python Shell and a script window open on a Raspberry Pi

1.02 Other Integrated Development Environments

IDLE is perfectly adequate for performing all the tasks required in this book. However, if you have been programming with IDLE for a number of years, you might like to try one of the other many IDEs available.

The one that is used for the remainder of the screenshots in this chapter, and occasionally later in the book, is Wing IDE 101 (Figure 1.04). This is a free version of a commercial IDE that provides a carefully selected set of facilities that are useful for students. It can be downloaded from http://wingware.com/downloads/wingide-101 where brief introductory videos and installation instructions are available. Please be aware that the Raspberry Pi is currently not powerful enough to run this or most other commercial IDEs satisfactorily. Wing IDE 101 is available for Windows, Apple computers, Ubuntu and other versions of Linux.

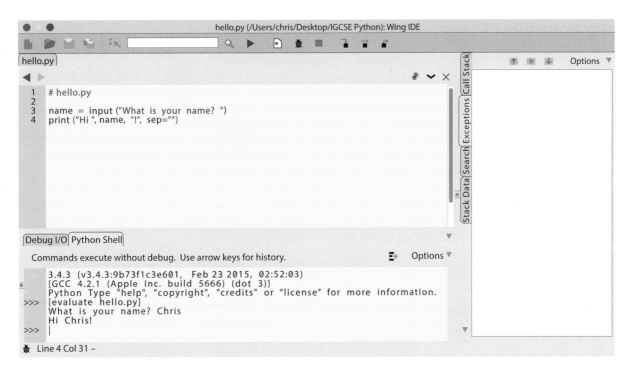

Figure 1.04 Wing IDE 101 Integrated Development Environment.

The large panel in the middle of the application is where you write your scripts. Interactive sessions can be run in the Shell tab below this window.

There are two ways to run a program in Wing IDE. Clicking the run button (▶) will access the Python Shell as shown in Figure 1.04. An alternative – and recommended – way of running your scripts is to click on the bug (🐞) to the right of the run button (Figure 1.05) This opens the Debug I/O panel and now provides error messages in the Exceptions tab on the right.

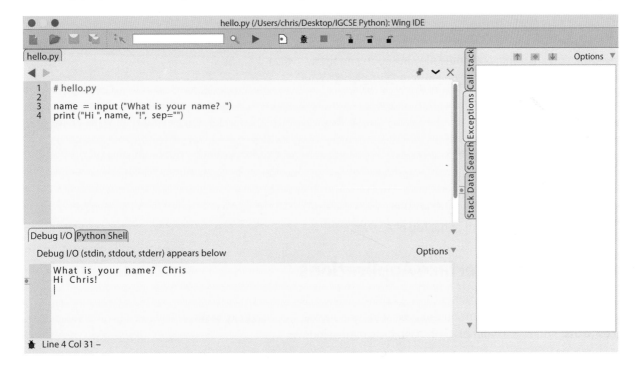

Figure 1.05 Wing IDE 101 showing input and output after pressing the bug button

5

1.03 Make Your First Program Using Interactive Mode

In IDLE's interactive mode window or in the Python Shell tab in Wing IDE, type out the following line of code at the >>> prompt and then press return.

```
INTERACTIVE SESSION

>>> print('Hello world!')
```

You have now run your first interactive mode program. Your code told the computer to print the text 'Hello world!' to the screen. It executed your code when you pressed the return key on your keyboard. You can also use interactive mode as a simple calculator. Try entering this sum and press return:

```
INTERACTIVE SESSION

>>> 3*4
```

> **TIP**
> Interactive sessions are used to illustrate simple concepts or to show the correct use of some new syntax. It is a good idea to start your own interactive session and try the code yourself. You may well want to experiment further to deepen your understanding.

1.04 Make Your First Program Using Script Mode

Working in IDLE select _New File_ from the _File_ menu to open a new window into which you can type your code and then save it as a script. In Wing IDE, simply type into the main script panel. Whichever IDE you are using, copy the following code and then save your file as **hello.py** to a new folder called _Python Code_ in your _Documents_ folder.

```
# hello.py
print('Hello world!')
```

If using IDLE, run the script by selecting _Run Module_ from the _Run_ menu or by pressing F5. In Wing IDE click the bug button.

Any code preceded by a hash symbol (#) is called a comment. This is ignored by the computer when executing the script and is purely for the programmer. It can be useful to include the file name in its own comment at the top of a script.

1.05 Graphical user interface Applications

Although not required by the syllabus, your Python scripts are not limited to text-based applications. By importing the **tkinter** module, it is easy to produce visually rich **graphical user interfaces** (**GUIs**) and attach your algorithms to buttons in windows.

Producing GUI based applications is outside the syllabus.

tkinter: An example of a GUI toolkit which is provided as part of the standard library when you install Python.

graphical user interface (GUI): Graphical user interfaces contain items like buttons, text entry boxes and radio buttons.

Chapter 5, GUI applications, is an optional chapter included in this book. In it, you will learn how to build your own GUIs and how to repurpose your algorithm solutions to work with them. From Chapter 5 onwards, there will be some tasks provided that include making GUIs. Although these are not required by the Cambridge IGCSE and O Level Computer Science syllabus, repurposing your solutions to work with GUIs will make you a more flexible programmer and allow you to produce more professional looking applications.

1.06 Additional Support

The intention of this book is to introduce programming concepts that make use of the non-language-specific formats included in the syllabus. Python 3 is used to provide the opportunity for you to use a real programming language to develop your understanding of these concepts. The official documentation for the Python programming language can be accessed at https://docs.python.org/3/.

A simple syntax reference guide that can be printed out and fits in your pocket is available from the Coding Club website at http://codingclub.co.uk/codecards/.

Further resources can be downloaded from cambridge.org/9781316617823.

Summary

- Python 3 is a loosely typed programming language that is designed to encourage easily read code.

- Python 3 comes with a simple Integrated Development Environment called IDLE.

- There are many other IDEs available, such as Wing IDE 101, which is specifically designed for students.

- There are three main styles of programming in Python 3:
    - interactive mode: quick tests and trials that can be programmed in the Python Shell
    - text-based: in script mode, text-based scripts can be saved so that your applications can be reused
    - GUI applications: full, visually rich applications that can be produced in script mode.

Chapter 2:
Sequence

Learning objectives

By the end of this chapter you will:

- know the difference between the three programming constructs: sequence, selection and iteration
- understand the role of flowcharts and pseudocode when designing programs
- understand the main symbols used in flowcharts
- understand the preferred format of pseudocode when using sequence solutions.

2.01 Logical Design Considerations

When designing programs, it is crucial to consider the order in which the task needs to be completed. All tasks will follow some logical order. When working on a solution to a problem, you should first apply the **top-down design** technique to break down the big problem into smaller ones. In terms of computational thinking, this is referred to as **decomposition**.

KEY TERMS

Top-down design: Design process where a complex task is broken down into smaller tasks.
Decomposition: The process of breaking down a large task into smaller tasks.

For example, to calculate the time it would take to complete a journey, you need to know the distance to be travelled and the intended speed. The first step would be to calculate the distance to be travelled. Without this **data** the rest of the task could not be completed.

The **sequence** in which instructions are programmed can be crucial. Consider the following algorithm:

```
Distance = Speed * Time
Speed = 12 kilometres per hour
Time = 15 minutes
```

KEY TERMS

Data: Raw facts and figures.
Sequence: Code is executed in the order it is written.

A human would recognise that the values for speed and time have been given after the calculation. A coded program would simply try to complete the task in the order given and crash. This is because at the time of the calculation no values have been provided for speed or time. In fact, the variables Speed and Time will not even be recognised by the program at this first step.

A human would probably also recognise that the speed is quoted 'per hour' while the time is given in minutes. They would be able to correctly calculate the distance as 3 kilometres (12 * 15/60). Even if the values had been provided before the calculation, the program would calculate distance incorrectly as 180 kilometres by simply multiplying the given values (12 * 15).

2.02 Programming Constructs

Python and other procedural languages make use of three basic programming constructs: sequence, **selection** and **iteration**. Combining these constructs provides a programmer with the tools required to solve logical problems. Selection and iteration offer a number of alternative approaches and are covered in detail in Chapters 6 and 7.

KEY TERMS

Selection: Code branches and follows a different sequence based on decisions made by the program.
Iteration: Code repeats a certain sequence of code a number of times depending on certain conditions.

9

Sequence

The order in which a process is completed is often crucial. Take the mathematical expression $A + B \times C + D$. The rules of precedence state that the multiply operation must be completed first. If a programmer wishes that the operations $A + B$ and $C + D$ be completed before multiplying, then it would be necessary to either complete the two additions separately first or write the expression in the form $(A + B) \times (C + D)$.

In programming, the sequence is indicated by the order in which the code is written, usually top to bottom. The program will execute the first line of code before moving to the second and subsequent lines.

Sequence is the subject of this chapter so this will be discussed in more detail later.

Selection

Often your programs will perform different processes dependent on user input. Consider a system designed to provide access to the school network based on when a user inputs a username and password. The system would need to follow a different path if the user inputs an incorrect password or username. In this circumstance, the user might simply be prompted to re-input their details. See Chapter 6 for more details.

Iteration

It is common for a program to perform identical processes on different data items. Consider a program that takes a series of coordinates and produces a line graph. The code that provides the instructions that plot each new coordinate will be repeated for each of the coordinates given. To repeat instructions, we put them in a loop, which is referred to as iteration. See Chapter 7 for more details.

2.03 Design Tools

When you design programs, it is normal to plan the logic of the program before you start to code the solution. This is an important step in the design of effective systems because a flaw in the logic will often result in programs that run but produce unexpected outputs.

The first step in the design process is to break down the problem into smaller problems. This is called top-down design. It makes it easier to plan and write code for these smaller problems. A **structure diagram** is used to help organise the top-down design. Chapter 8 provides more detail about top-down design and structure diagrams.

The next stage is to design an algorithm for the individual problems. Two approaches that can be used at this stage to help generate logically accurate systems are **flowcharts** and **pseudocode**.

 KEY TERMS

Structure diagrams: A diagrammatical method of expressing a system as a series of subsystems.
Flowchart: A graphical representation of the logic of a system.
Pseudocode: A language-independent system for defining the logic of a system without the need for strict syntax.

To succeed in your course, you will be expected to have a working understanding of flowcharts and pseudocode. You will need to be able to use them to explain the logic of your solutions to given tasks. Both methods are used throughout this book.

Problem solving and design: use flowcharts and pseudocode.

2.04 Flowcharts

Flowcharts are graphical representations of the logic of the intended system. They make use of symbols to represent operations or processes and are joined by lines indicating the sequence of operations. Table 2.01 details the symbols used.

Table 2.01

Symbol	Notes	Example
Terminator	The START or END of a system.	START END
Input or output	Use when INPUT is required from the user or OUTPUT is being sent to the user.	INPUT number OUTPUT result
Process	A process within the system. Beware of making the process too generic. For example, a process entitled 'Calculate Average' would be too generic. It needs to indicate the values used to calculate the average.	result ←A * B average ← (A+B+C+D)/4
Data flow line	Joins two operations. The arrowhead indicates the direction of the flow. Iteration (looping) can be indicated by arrows returning to an earlier process in the flowchart.	INPUT A, B result ←A * B OUTPUT result
Decision	A point in the sequence where alternative paths can be taken The condition is written within the symbol. Where multiple alternatives exist, this is indicated by chained decision symbols. Each 'No' condition directs to another decision in the process.	Yes ← number > 10 ? → No No ← input = A ? → Yes input = B ? → Yes No ← input = C ? → Yes

11

2.05 Pseudocode

Pseudocode is a method of describing the logic and sequence of a system. It uses keywords and constructs similar to those used in programming languages but without the strict use of syntax required by formal languages. It allows the logic of the system to be defined in a language-independent format. This can then be coded using any programming language. Hence, the flow diagrams and pseudocode in this book are almost entirely the same as those used in the Visual Basic sister book of the series.

Pseudocode follows a number of underlying principles:

- Use capital letters for keywords close to those used in programming languages.

- Use lower case letters for natural language descriptions.

- Use indentation to show the start and end of blocks of code statements, primarily when using selection and iteration.

One of the advantages of learning to program using Python is that the actual coding language is structured in a similar way to natural language and therefore closely resembles pseudocode. Python IDEs such as IDLE or Wing IDE also automatically indent instructions where appropriate.

SYLLABUS CHECK

Pseudocode: understand and use pseudocode for assignment, using ←.

2.06 Pseudocode Example

The following pseudocode is for an algorithm that accepts the input of two numbers. These values are added together and the result is stored in a memory area called `answer`. The value in `answer` is then displayed to the user. (In Chapter 3, we will learn that this memory area is known as a variable.)

```
INPUT number1
INPUT number2
answer ← number1 + number2
OUTPUT answer
```

Note the use of ← to show the passing of values. This is pseudocode's assignment operator. In pseudocode the equals symbol (=) is used to compare values. It is important to note that in Python the equals symbol is used for assignment and two equals symbols (==) are used to compare values.

TASK

Task 1
Construct a flowchart to represent this pseudocode example.

2.07 Effective use of Flowcharts and Pseudocode

Due to their universal nature, flowcharts and pseudocode are used extensively in the Cambridge IGCSE and O Level Computer Science syllabus.

The aim of this book is to help you to learn how to code effective systems in Python. The following chapters make use of flowcharts and pseudocode to define the logic of systems before moving on to specific Python solutions.

TIP

After completing a flowchart or pseudocode, it is a good idea to try and follow it through a step at a time in the same way a computer would in order to identify if you have any missing steps.

Learning how to explain the logic of programs by using these design techniques is important not only in your preparation for examination but also for your preparation in using the languages of the future. Language syntax is likely to change but the need for effective computational thinking will remain.

Summary

- Programmers make use of three constructs when writing code:
  - sequence: the logical order in which code is executed
  - selection: branching of code onto different paths based on certain conditions
  - iteration: repetition of sections of code.
- Before coding a program, it is crucial to design an appropriate algorithm.
- Flowcharts are graphical representations of the logic of a system. They make use of symbols to represent operations or processes, and lines indicate the sequence of operations.
- Pseudocode describes the logic of a system in a similar way to a programming language but without such strict syntax requirements.

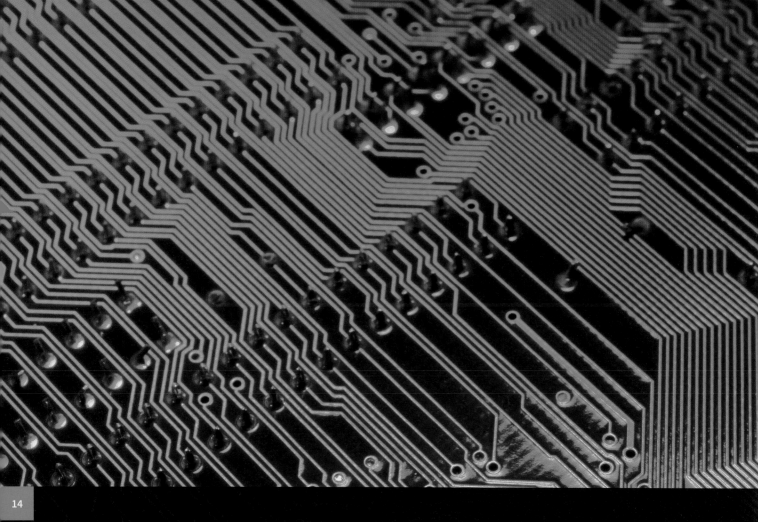

Chapter 3:
Variables and Arithmetic Operators

Learning objectives

By the end of this chapter you will understand how to:

- declare and use variables and constants
- use the data types Integer, Real, Char, String and Boolean
- use basic mathematical operators to process input values
- design and represent simple programs using flowcharts and pseudocode.

3.01 Variables and Constants

Programs are normally designed to accept and input data, and process that data to produce the required output. Data used in programs can vary depending on the aim of the program; a calculator will process numerical data while a program designed to check email addresses will process textual data. When writing programs, you will use variables or constants to refer to these data values. A **variable** identifies data that can be changed during the execution of a program while a **constant** is used for data values that remain fixed. In many computer languages, the **data type** must be provided when a variable or constant is declared. The data type is used by the computer to allocate a suitable location in memory. These languages, such as Java, are said to be strongly typed.

KEY TERMS

Variable: The identifier (name) given to a memory location used to store data; the value can be changed during program execution.

Constant: A named memory location that contains data that can be read but not changed by the program. (In Python, the data can be changed. However, by capitalising your variable name, you are indicating to readers of your code the intention that the value of the data should not be.)

Data type: The format of the data in the field.

Python is an example of a loosely typed programming language. In Python, all variables are in actual fact objects. The computer decides on a variable's data type from the context you provide. Compare these two variable declarations, first in Visual Basic and then in Python:

In Visual Basic:

```
Dim Score As Integer = 0
```

In Python:

```
score = 0
```

3.02 Types of Data

If Python decides which data types are required for the programmer, how can we know what data type has been allocated? This is achieved by using the built in `type()` function. Study this interactive session in the Python Shell to see how to use this function:

```
INTERACTIVE SESSION

>>> my_integer = 3
>>> type(my_integer)
<class 'int'>
>>> my_string = 'hello'
>>> type(my_string)
<class 'str'>
```

The basic data types you need to know are identified in Table 3.01.

Table 3.01

Data type	Description and use	Python `type(variable)` query returns:
Integer	Whole numbers, either positive or negative Used with quantities such as the number of students at a school – you cannot have half a student.	`'int'`
Real	Positive or negative fractional values Used with numerical values that require decimal parts, such as currency. Real is the data type used by many programming languages and is also referred to in the Cambridge IGCSE and O Level Computer Science syllabus.	`'float'` Python does not use the term Real. The equivalent data type in Python is called 'floating point'.

Char	A single character or symbol (for example A, z, $, 6)
	
	A Char variable that holds a digit, cannot be used in calculations.
		`'str'`
		
		Python treats characters as small Strings.
		
		Note:
		
		`>>> my_var = '3'`
		`>>> type(my_var)`
		`<class 'str'>`
		`>>> my_var = 3`
		`>>> type(my_var)`
		`<class 'int'>`

String	More than one character (a String of characters) Used to hold words, names or sentences.	`'str'`

Boolean	One of two values, either True or False
	
	Used to indicate the result of a condition. For example, in a computer game, a Boolean variable might be used to store whether a player has chosen to have the sound effects on.
		`'bool'`
		
		e.g.
		
		`>>> sfx = False`
		`>>> type(sfx)`
		`<class 'bool'>`

SYLLABUS CHECK

Programming concepts: understand and use Integer, Real, Char, String and Boolean.

3.03 Pseudo Numbers

Telephone numbers and ISBNs both consist of digits but are not truly numbers. They are only a collection of digits used to uniquely identify an item; sometimes they contain spaces or start with a zero. They are not intended to be used in calculations. These are known as pseudo numbers and it is normal to store then in a String variable. If you store a mobile phone number as an Integer, any leading zeroes will be removed and spaces and symbols are not permitted.

3.04 Naming Conventions in Python

There are a variety of naming conventions in Python. Here are a few of them:

Variable Names

Use all lower case, starting with a letter and joining words with underscores. It is considered good practice to use descriptive names as this aids readability and reduces the need for so much commenting.

For example:

```
score_total = 56    ✓
Total = 56          ✗
t = 56              ✗
```

> **FURTHER INFORMATION**
>
> There are 31 reserved words that cannot be used as your own variable names:
>
> ```
> and as assert break class continue def del elif else except
> finally for from global if import in is lambda nonlocal not or
> pass print raise return try while with yield.
> ```

Constants

Use all upper case characters to indicate constants.

For example:

```
PI = 3.1415
```

It is considered good practice to give global variables an initial value when **declaring variables**: this is known as **initialising variables**. See the next section for more about global and local variables.

KEY TERMS

Declaring variables: When a variable is given a name and assigned no value. It is important to declare or initialise global variables.

Initialising variables: When a variable is given a start value.

3.05 Variable Scope

When declaring a variable, the placement of the declaration in the code will determine which elements of the program are able to make use of the variable.

Global variables are those that can be accessed from any routine within the program. To give a variable global status, it must be declared outside any specific subroutine. It is good practice to make all the global variable declarations at the start of your code directly below any import statements.

To access global variables in functions, they can be called as normal; however, if the function is going to change the value stored in the global variable it must be re-declared using the `global` keyword (see example on page 18).

Variable Scope is outside the syllabus

17

Local variables can only be accessed in the code element in which they are declared. They are used when the use of the variable will be limited to a single routine such as a function. Using local variables reduces the possibility of accidentally changing variable values in other parts of your program.

KEY TERMS

Global variables: Variables that can be accessed from any routine within the program.

Local variables: Variables that can only be accessed in the code element in which they are declared.

In the following Python code example, there is a global variable (`player_score`) and one local variable (`result`) As the value of the global variable might be changed by the `update_player_score()` function, `player_score` needs to be re-declared at the start of the function with the `global` keyword:

```
player_score = 0

def update_player_score():
    global player_score
    result = 5
    if player_score < result:
        player_score = player_score+1
```

18

3.06 Arithmetic Operators

There are a number of operations that can be performed on numerical data. Combining these operations and appropriate variables allows you to create programs that are capable of performing numerical computational tasks.

The basic operators used in Python 3 are shown in Table 3.02

Table 3.02

Operation	Example of use	Description
Addition	`result = number1 + number2`	Adds the values held in the variables `number1` and `number2` and stores the result in the variable `result`.
Subtraction	`result = number1 - number2`	Subtracts the value held in `number2` from the value in `number1` and stores the result in the variable `result`.
Multiplication	`result = number1 * number2`	Multiplies the values held in the variables `number1` and `number2` and stores the result in the variable `result`.
Division	`result = number1 / number2`	Divides the value held in the variable `number1` by the value held in `number2` and stores the result in the variable `result`.
Integer division	`result = number1 // number2`	Finds the number of times `number2` can go into `number1` completely, discards the remainder, and stores the result in the variable `result`.

TIP

If you find yourself having to write some Python 2 programs, it is important to be aware that the syntax for division and Integer division is the other way around.

Now is a good time to open up a Python Shell and have an interactive session to try out some of these operators yourself. To get you started, try completing these two interactive sessions by pressing return after the final line in each case. Don't forget to find out what value is stored in c as well.

> INTERACTIVE SESSION
>
> ```
> >>> a = 7
> >>> b = 3
> >>> c = a/b
> >>> type(c)
> ```

TASK

Task 1

How can you find out what value is stored in c?

> INTERACTIVE SESSION
>
> ```
> >>> a = 7
> >>> b = 3
> >>> c = a//b
> >>> type(c)
> ```

19

3.07 Programming Tasks

DEMO TASK

Multiply Machine

Produce a system called Multiply Machine that takes two numbers inputted by the user. It then multiplies them together and outputs the result.

TIP

Whenever you are provided with a demo task, it is a good idea to open a new file in script mode and copy in the code provided. Think about what each line of code is doing as you type. Then save the script and try it out.

First you need to design the algorithm. Figure 3.01 shows flowchart and pseudocode solutions for the task.

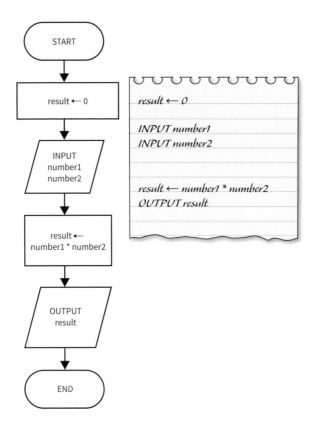

Figure 3.01 Flowchart and pseudocode for multiplication algorithm.

In Python, assignment is indicated by the use of the = symbol. In pseudocode the ← is used.

SYLLABUS CHECK

Pseudocode: understand and use pseudocode commands INPUT and OUTPUT.

TIP

You will want to use Python's `input()` function to send a message to the user and collect their keyboard input. Remember that `input()` only returns String data types, so if you need to do calculations on numbers supplied by your user, you will have to **cast** the String into an Integer by using the `int()` function.

For example:

```
age = int(input('How old are you?'))
```

Here is a Python implementation of the solution from Figure 3.01:

```
# multiply_demo.py

# Request and store user input
number1 = int(input('Please insert first number: '))
number2 = int(input('Please insert second number: '))

result = number1 * number2

# Display the value held in the variable result
print('The answer is ', result)

# End nicely by waiting for the user to press the return key.
input('/n/nPress RETURN to finish.')
```

KEY TERMS

Casting: The process of changing the data type of a given variable into another data type. For example, a variable that holds the string value '2' could be cast into an integer variable storing the value 2.

TASKS

Task 2 – Addition Machine

Amend the Multiply Machine replacing multiplication with addition.

Will all the numerical values remain Integer data types throughout the life of the application?

Task 3 – Volume of Water in Aquarium

Design a program where the inputs will be the height, width and depth of an aquarium. The output should be the number of litres of water that the aquarium will hold ($1\,l = 1000\,cm^3$).

Task 4 – Area and Circumference of a Circle

A system takes the radius of a circle as its input and calculates the area of the circle and its circumference.

1   Draw a flowchart and create a pseudocode algorithm that will output the area of the circle and the circumference based on the input radius.

2   Test that your algorithm works by programming and running the code in Python.

3.08 Development Challenges

Challenge yourself, or your fellow students, to complete a programming task. The following are some examples of the type of task you might like to consider. The last two are complex mathematical challenges.

For each challenge, you should draw a flowchart and create a pseudocode algorithm before programming and running the code in Python.

Task 5

Program a system that takes as inputs:

- The length of the base of a triangle.
- The perpendicular height of the triangle.

The system should output the area of the triangle.

Task 6

Program a system that takes as inputs:

- The average speed of a car over the length of a journey.
- The distance that the car has to travel.

The system should output, in minutes, the length of time the journey will take.

Task 7

Program a system that takes the three inputs required to calculate the area of a trapezoid and outputs the area.

Task 8

Program a system that takes the length of one side of a regular octagon and outputs the resultant area of the octagon.

Hint: To take a square root of a number in Python use this code: `number**0.5`

Summary

- Programs use variables and constants to hold values.
- Variables and constants have identifiers (names) which are used to refer to them in the program.
- Variables are able to have the value they contain changed during the execution of a program. The values within constants remain the same while the program is running.
- In Python, variable names should be descriptive and consist of lower case words joined by underscores.
- In Python, constant names should contain all capital letters. In Cambridge IGCSE and O Level Computer Science pseudocode, they should be preceded with the CONSTANT keyword.
- It is important to know what data types your variables are using. This can be checked by using the `type()` function in Python.
- The `input()` function returns values from the user as String data types. If number inputs are required, the values returned must be cast into Integers or Floats using the `int()` or `float()` functions.
- Mathematical operators can be used with values held in numeric variables.
- Local variables are those that are declared inside a subroutine (see Chapter 4). They cannot be accessed by the rest of the program.
- Global variables are accessed by all parts of a program and are often initialised near the top of a script.
- When designing algorithms, it is crucial to consider the logical sequence of execution. It is important to declare and initialise global variables as well as obtaining user input before completing any processing that requires them.

Chapter 4:
Subroutines

Learning objectives

By the end of this chapter you will understand:

- how subroutines are used in programming
- how values are passed to and received from subroutines
- how to design, program and use a function
- how to design, program and use a procedure.

4.01 Subroutines

A subroutine is a sequence of program code that performs a specific task but does not represent the entire system.

All subroutines in Python require a name and the keyword `def` which is short for define.

When a subroutine is activated (this is referred to as 'called'), the calling program is halted and control is transferred to the subroutine. After the subroutine has completed execution, control is passed back to the calling program. This modularised approach to programming brings with it advantages over a simple sequenced program.

Consider a GUI program that maintains its running status while waiting for various subroutines to be called by activation of event triggers. The subroutines execute their code and pass control back to the main program.

This allows the programmer to generate the complete program from a series of individual subroutines. Some code is executed when the script is loaded, other elements when certain buttons are clicked and possibly further elements of code are activated when text is changed in a text box. Imagine the complexity of the program code if only a single sequence of code was available to the programmer.

24

Advantages of Using Subroutines

The ability to call subroutines from the main code offers a number of advantages:

- The subroutine can be called when needed: A single block of code can be used many times in the entire program, avoiding the need for repeating identical code sequences throughout. This improves the modularity of the code, makes it easier to understand and helps in the identification of errors.

- There is only one section of code to debug: If an error is located in a subroutine, only the individual subroutine needs to be debugged. Had the code been repeated throughout the main program, each occurrence would need to be altered.

- There is only one section of code to update: Improvements and extensions of the code are available everywhere the subroutine is called.

Types of Subroutine

Two main types of subroutine exist:

- **Procedures** are small sections of code that can be reused. They do not return a value. In pseudocode, a procedure is named and takes the form:

```
PROCEDURE ... ENDPROCEDURE.
```

They are called by using the CALL statement.

- **Functions** are similar to procedures. The difference is that functions have one or more values passed to them and one or more values are returned to the main program after they have completed running. In pseudocode, a function takes the form:

> *FUNCTION(values to be passed in) . . . ENDFUNCTION.*

The CALL statement is used to execute the function but the values required must be passed to the function at the same time:

> *CALL my_function(values required by the function)*

KEY TERMS

Procedure: A small section of code that can run repeatedly from different parts of the program.
Function: A procedure that returns a value.

4.02 Programming a Function

The syntax for defining a function in Python is shown here:

```
def circle(r):
    # code to draw a circle goes here
```

To draw a circle of radius ten in the main part of the program we would write:

```
circle(10)
```

Notice how the radius has been passed to the function at call time and there is no need to use a CALL keyword as is used in Cambridge IGCSE and O Level Computer Science pseudocode; the function name suffices in Python.

25

Programming a Function is outside the syllabus

Passing Parameters to a Procedure

The passing of parameters can be very useful. For example, a procedure to check network logon details could take the parameters **username** and **password**. Having checked the data against the logon database, it could return **True** or **False** to indicate if the details match records, or **'update password'** if the password has expired. The procedure could be called repeatedly and passed different parameters every time a user attempts to log on.

DEMO TASK

Multiples

A function is required that will be passed an Integer and output the first five multiples of that value.

The pseudocode for this function and its call from the main program are as shown here:

```
FUNCTION multiples(number)
    FOR i = 1 TO 5
        OUTPUT number * i
    NEXT
ENDFUNCTION

CALL multiples(10)
```

This uses a **FOR loop**. FOR loops are introduced more fully in Chapter 7.

 KEY TERMS

FOR loop: A type of iteration that will repeat a section of code a known number of times.

TASK

Task 1

Create a pseudocode algorithm for an amended version of the Multiples procedure that accepts two parameters: a number to use as the multiplier and another to indicate the maximum number of multiplications required.

26

Functions That Return Values to the Calling Routine

Often programmers write functions that are required to produce answers for repetitive tasks and then return those values to the main program. For example, it might be necessary for a program to calculate the circumference of several circles from their radii.

DEMO TASK

Circumference

A function is required that will be passed the radius of a circle and return the circumference.

The pseudocode for this function and its call from the main program are as shown below.

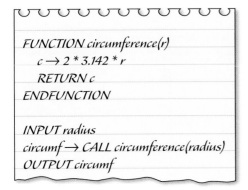

```
FUNCTION circumference(r)
    c → 2 * 3.142 * r
    RETURN c
ENDFUNCTION

INPUT radius
circumf → CALL circumference(radius)
OUTPUT circumf
```

Here is a Python implementation:

```python
def circumference(r):
    c = 2 * 3.142 * r
    return c

radius = int(input('What is the radius of your circle? '))

circumf = circumference(radius)
print('The circumference of your circle is', circumf)
```

Note how the function is not activated by use of the keyword CALL in Python. The name of the function is used as a variable in an assignment statement. Each time the name is used, the function is executed and the return value placed in the variable or output indicated.

TASK

Task 2

Create a pseudocode algorithm for an amended version of this function that, when passed the radius, returns the area of a circle.

Test that your algorithm works by programming and running the code in Python.

Returning Two Values from a Function

It is easy to return two values in pseudocode:

```
RETURN value1, value2
```

In Python, this is accomplished in the same way. Look at this interactive session to see how this works:

```
INTERACTIVE SESSION

>>> def my_function():
        return 1,2

>>> a,b = my_function()
>>> print(a)
1
>>> print(b)
2
>>>
```

TASK

Task 3

Create a pseudocode and flowchart algorithm for an amended version of the circumference function. When passed the radius, this function returns the area and the circumference of a circle.

Test that your algorithm works by programming and running the code in Python.

4.03 Programming a Procedure

The Python code for a procedure is similar to that used for a function. In this case empty brackets are used to show that no parameters are required by the subroutine. See how this works in the interactive session shown below:

Programming a Procedure is outside the syllabus

```
INTERACTIVE SESSION

>>> def greeting():
        print('Hello', 'Hello', 'Hello')
>>> greeting()
Hello Hello Hello
>>>
```

Notice how the `greeting()` function contains the built-in function, `print()`.

TASK

Task 4

a Create a pseudocode algorithm for a procedure called **dead_end**() that prints out 'I am sorry, you can go no further this way!' This might then be called in a maze game whenever a player reaches the end of a passage.

b Test that your algorithm works by programming the procedure in Python and providing a call to the procedure.

Summary

- Subroutines provide an independent section of code that can be called when needed from another routine while the program is running. In this way subroutines can be used to perform common tasks within a program.

- As an independent section of code, a subroutine is easier to debug, maintain or update than repetitive code within the main program.

- Subroutines are called from another routine. Once they have completed execution they pass control back to the calling routine.

- Subroutines can be passed values known as parameters.

- A procedure is used to separate out repetitive code from the main program.

- A function is a type of subroutine which can receive multiple parameters and return values.

Chapter 5:
GUI Applications (Optional)

Learning objectives

By the end of this chapter you will understand:

- how to produce and save GUI applications
- how to program windowed applications using the built-in tkinter GUI module
- how to add widgets to a GUI application
- how to lay out widgets in an application window
- how to trigger function calls with buttons.

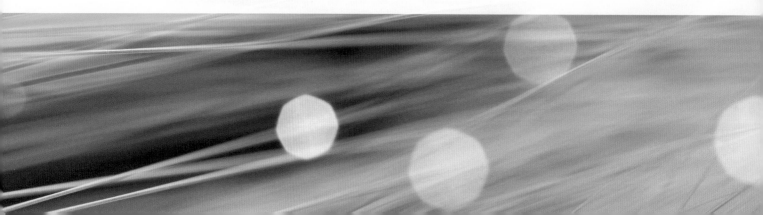

5.01 Introduction

In Chapter 1, you were introduced to interactive mode and script-based programming. This optional chapter shows you how to create programs that appear in windows and have features such as buttons and text boxes. The Cambridge IGCSE and O Level Computer Science syllabus does not require that you produce applications with GUIs; however, you may well want to produce more visually interesting and professional looking solutions to problems. Doing so will also make you a more flexible programmer as you reformat your scripts into GUI applications.

From now on, normal script-based solutions are going to be referred to as text-based solutions and programs that appear in windows are going to be called GUI solutions. After this chapter, you will often be asked to produce two solutions, first a text-based one and then a GUI solution. Producing the GUI programs can be considered optional extensions.

Producing GUI based applications is outside the syllabus.

5.02 Make Your First Application in a Window with a Button

By importing the tkinter module, it is easy to produce visually rich GUIs and attach your algorithms to buttons in windows.

Tkinter is an example of a GUI toolkit and is provided as part of the standard library when you install Python. Therefore, you already have access to the objects and methods required to make GUI applications, and you just need to do these extra tasks:

1 Import the *tkinter* module.

2 Create the main tkinter window.

3 Add one or more tkinter **widgets** to your application.

4 Enter the main event loop, which listens to and acts upon events triggered by the user.

KEY TERMS

widget: Interface items such as buttons and text boxes that can be used to build GUIs.

A button can call for a particular action to happen by referring to a function by name after `command=` in the button definition code. To create the application shown in Figure 5.01 copy the code into a new script and save it as `hello-gui.py` into your Python Code folder:

31

```
# hello-gui.py

# Import everything required from the tkinter module
from tkinter import *

# Function called by clicking my_button:
def change_text():
    my_label.config(text='Hello World')

# Create the main tkinter window
window = Tk()
window.title('My Application')

# Add an empty tkinter label widget and place it in a grid layout
my_label = Label(window, width=25, height=1, text='')
my_label.grid(row=0, column=0)

# Add a tkinter button widget, place it in the grid layout
# and attach the change_text() function
my_button = Button(window, text='Say Hi', width=10, command=change_text)
my_button.grid(row=1, column=0)

# Enter the main event loop
window.mainloop()
```

Figure 5.01 A GUI application with a button

After running the code, press the 'Say Hi' button to see how this small application works. Notice how the button is linked to the `change_text()` function by `command=` in the button definition.

FURTHER INFORMATION

The tkinter module provides classes, objects and methods that you can access and use in your own applications. Tkinter is written using object-oriented programming (OOP), which is beyond the scope of the syllabus. In OOP programs, object methods are accessed using the dot operator. This can be seen above in the `change_text()` function where the `config()` method is applied to the label widget.

If you want to learn more about OOP you might like to work through *Python: Building Big Apps*, a level 3 book in the Coding Club series, or perhaps try *Introduction to Programming with Greenfoot* by Michael Kölling, which teaches Java programming in a very interactive, game-based way. It is worth noting that while the syllabus focuses on solving problems through a top-down design process, discussed in detail in Chapter 8, OOP is a good example of how to solve problems through bottom-up design.

When laying out GUI applications, you can use the `grid()` method, which organises as many cells as you require in your window using a coordinate system. Note how the numbers start from zero in the top left corner of the window:

row=0, column=0	row=0, column=1	row=0, column=2
row=1, column=0	row=1, column=1	row=1, column=2
row=2, column=0	row=2, column=1	row=2, column=2

It is possible to further arrange tkinter widgets by grouping them in frames.

5.03 Other Tkinter Widgets You Can Use in Your Applications

Below are a few other useful widget examples you might want to include in your applications. These code snippets should all be added after `window = Tk()` and above `window.mainloop()` as indicated by the comment in the following recipe for an empty tkinter window:

```
from tkinter import *

window = Tk()
window.title('My Application')

# widget code goes here

window.mainloop()
```

A text entry box with a label:

```
Label(window, text='Name:').grid(row=0, column=0)
my_text_box = Entry(window, width=15)
my_text_box.grid(row=0, column=1)
```

Two frames:

```
frame1 = Frame(window,height=20,width=100,bg='green')
frame1.grid(row=0, column=0)
frame2 = Frame(window,height=20,width=100,bg='red')
frame2.grid(row=1, column=1)
```

A drop-down menu:

```
options = (1,2,3)
my_variable_object = IntVar() # access the value with .get()
my_variable_object.set('choose:')
my_dropdown = OptionMenu(window, my_variable_object, *options)
my_dropdown.grid()
```

TIP
When programming graphical implementations of tasks set in future chapters, remember to consult the Appendix where you will find a full set of recipes for the widgets you will be asked to use.

TASK

Task 1 – Tkinter Widgets

Open a new script and add the code from the empty window recipe on page 33. Save this script and then add the code for the example widgets, one at a time, to see how they appear. Do not worry about your scripts doing anything at this stage.

DEMO TASK

Gender GUI Application

Create a radio button application that gives the user a choice of two radio buttons to indicate their gender. Your application should show how to align tkinter widgets to the left (West) side of a `grid()` cell. It should also demonstrate how to access the value selected in the radio buttons using a tkinter `StringVar()` object and display the choice made (Figure 5.02).

TIP

When building GUI applications, it is good practice to separate the logic from the design. To do this, compartmentalise your algorithm solutions into functions at the top of your script and then build your GUI code at the bottom of your script.

Here is the Python code that demonstrates how to produce a GUI for this very simple one function program.

```python
# gender-gui.py

from tkinter import *

# Functions go here:
def change_text():
    my_label.config(text=gender.get())

# GUI code goes here:
# Create the main tkinter window
window = Tk()
window.title('My Application')

# Add an empty tkinter label widget and place it in a grid layout
my_label = Label(window, width=25, height=1, text='')
my_label.grid(row=0, column=0)

# Add a tkinter button widget, place it in the grid layout
# and attach the change_text() function
my_button = Button(window, text='Submit', width=10, command=change_text)
my_button.grid(row=1, column=0)

# Create a tkinter string variable object for the radio buttons
gender = StringVar()
```

```
# Add two radio button widgets
# Use optional sticky argument to align left
radio1 = Radiobutton(window, text='Female', variable=gender, value='female')
radio1.grid(row=2, column=0, sticky=W)
radio1.select() # pre-selects this radio button for the user
radio2 = Radiobutton(window, text='Male', variable=gender, value='male')
radio2.grid(row=3, column=0, sticky=W)

# Enter the main loop event
window.mainloop()
```

Figure 5.02 A GUI application with two radio buttons

TASK

Task 2 – Drop-down Menu

Rewrite the radio button application but replace the radio buttons with a simple drop-down menu.

5.04 Choosing a Text-based or GUI Application

From Chapter 6 onwards, answers to problems are given as either text-based applications or GUI applications and often both.

Text-based programs offer the benefit of more accurately reflecting the programming style of the syllabus and will help to prepare you for the A Level syllabus. Text-based applications do not involve the additional complexity of having to reference tkinter's GUI widgets.

However, GUI applications will offer a richer visual experience and produce systems similar to those commercially available.

It is suggested that you make use of both types of applications. This will best support the development of your computational thinking. A text-based answer is always provided to problems presented in this book in the final chapter, Chapter 14: Solutions. If a GUI-based solution makes sense, these are also provided in the code repository found at the companion website to this textbook at cambridge.org/9781316617823.

Summary

- There are three main styles of programming in Python 3:
  - interactive mode: quick tests and trials that can be programmed in the Python Shell
  - text-based: in script mode, text-based scripts can be saved so that your applications can be reused
  - GUI applications: by importing the tkinter library, full visually rich applications can be produced in script mode.
- GUI programs open in their own window and contain familiar widgets such as buttons and text boxes.
- The tkinter module is a GUI library that is available in the standard Python 3 install.
- Tkinter's grid method allows programmers to position widgets by using cell coordinates starting with (0,0) from the top left corner of a window or frame.
- Text-based programs are all that is required by the syllabus and closely match the logic of the algorithms they implement.
- GUI programs provide a richer experience for the user but introduce added complexity for the programmer.

Producing GUI based applications is outside the syllabus.

Chapter 6:
Selection

Learning objectives

By the end of this chapter you will understand:

- how selection can be used to allow a program to follow different paths of execution
- how selection is shown in flowcharts and pseudocode
- the differences between and the advantages of using:
  - IF . . . THEN . . . ELSE . . . ENDIF statements
  - IF . . . THEN . . . ELSE . . . ELSEIF . . . ENDIF statements
  - NESTED IF statements
  - CASE . . . OR . . . OTHERWISE . . . ENDCASE statements
- how to use logical operators when programming selection in algorithms.

6.01 The Need for Selection

Systems often need to be programmed to complete different processes depending on the input received. For example, an automatic door will open if it detects that someone wishes to enter and will shut when no presence is detected. Expert systems provide answers or conclusions based on the user response to previous questions. Systems like these appear to be able to make decisions based on input, but the reality is that the system has been logically designed to complete a certain process based on expected input.

In Python, and many other languages, this is achieved by the use of programming techniques known as **IF statements**. Many languages also have **CASE statements** available to them and, although Python does not, you will need to be familiar with this construct in your exams. When programming your solutions in Python, you will usually replace CASE statements with `if...elif...else` (see Section 6.08).

KEY TERMS

IF statements: A statement that allows the program to follow or ignore a sequence of code depending on the data being processed.

CASE statements: A statement that allows one of several sequences of code to be executed depending on the data being processed.

6.02 IF Statements

If the process for an automatic door was written down, it might appear as: 'If a presence is detected then open the door, otherwise close it.' In simple terms, this is very similar to coding an IF statement. The program will need to provide a condition to evaluate ('If a presence is detected') and two actions will need to be provided depending on whether the outcome is True or False: if True 'open the door', if False 'close the door'.

SYLLABUS CHECK

Pseudocode: understand and use pseudocode, using IF . . . THEN . . . ELSE . . . ENDIF.

In a flowchart, the symbol used to indicate a decision is a diamond. The diamond contains information about the criteria and normally has two exit routes indicating the True and False paths.

The flowchart in Figure 6.01(a) includes the decision symbol. The True and False paths have been indicated; when programmed this will become an IF statement. Once the appropriate action has been performed, the program flow returns back to 'Check for presence at door' and the input is again evaluated by the IF statement.

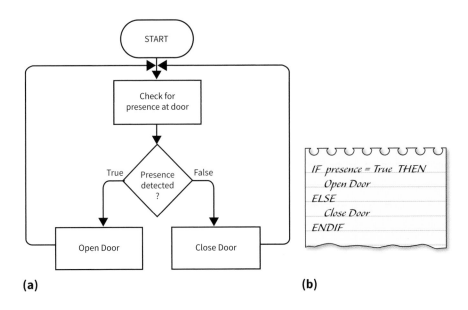

(a)   **(b)**

Figure 6.01 Flowchart (a) and pseudocode (b) for a decision

Note that True/False can also be written as Yes/No.

The pseudocode IF statement for the flowchart in Figure 6.01(a) is shown in Figure 6.01(b). The start of the statement is indicated by IF. The condition is written between IF and THEN. The action to be taken if the condition is True follows THEN. The action is indented to improve readability. ELSE indicates any alternative action. Again, the action to be taken should be indented. ENDIF indicates the end of the statement.

Not all IF statements have an alternative action and therefore the ELSE may be omitted. For example, a system used to calculate the cost of a train fare could apply a discount if the passenger is a child. The pseudocode would look like this:

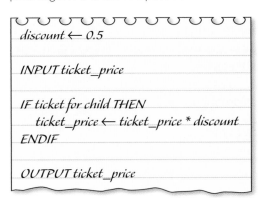

6.03 Logical Operators

In the automatic door example, the only possible inputs were 'detected' or 'not detected'. However, many systems depend on less discrete criteria. An air-conditioning system will receive continuous temperature data and will perform actions based on a variety of temperature data. A system for determining exam grades will calculate the grade output by identifying whether the students' marks fall within certain grade boundaries.

To support the needs of these types of decisions, a number of logical operators exist. They tend to follow the accepted mathematical use of operator symbols. The basic operators supported by Python and their form in pseudocode is shown in Table 6.01

Table 6.01

Operator description	Pseudocode	Python3
is equal to	=	==
is greater than	>	>
is less than	<	<
is greater than or equal to	>=	>=
is less than or equal to	<=	<=
is not equal to	!= or <>	! = <>

The choice of the correct logical operator is important. Using the wrong one can produce unexpected results in your algorithms. Often the way in which the decision required is worded will indicate the appropriate operator to use (Table 6.02).

Table 6.02

Decision in words	Appropriate operator
Apply a discount for students aged under 16	IF student < 16 THEN
Turn on the water cooler when the temperature is 10°C or more	IF temp >= 10 THEN

Chapter 10 provides you with techniques to identify logical errors such as selecting < when you should have used <=.

6.04 Coding IF Statements in Python

The code for an IF statement in Python is slightly different to that required in pseudocode. The Python programming language is designed to encourage programmers to write easily read code. Indentation of four spaces is required and implemented by IDEs to all blocks of code. Extraneous details sometimes found in other languages such as ending statements with semi-colons as well as a line return; wrapping code blocks in curly brackets as well as indenting and adding ENDIF statements as well as ending the indentation are all dropped. Note though that, unlike in pseudocode, a colon is used before indenting a block of code after, for example, an IF statement. This is to help IDEs to know when to start auto-indenting, and is consistent throughout the language.

DEMO TASK

Sort Two Numbers

Design a system that will take as input two whole numbers. If the second number is larger than the first, the system will output 'Second'; if not the output should be 'First' (Figure 6.02).

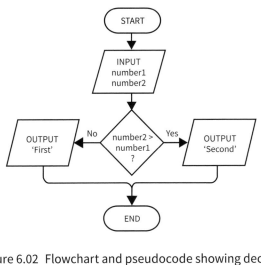
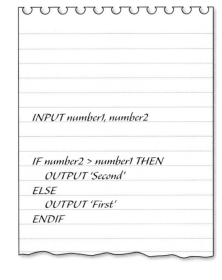

Figure 6.02 Flowchart and pseudocode showing decision

The Python code below implements the system designed in the flowchart and pseudocode shown in Figure 6.02:

```python
number1 = int(input('Enter first number: '))
number2 = int(input('Enter second number: '))

if number2 > number1:
    print('Second')
else:
    print('First')
```

TASKS

Task 1

Would the same output be achieved by reversing the condition to `number1 < number2`?

Task 2

The demo task has been reworded very slightly like this:

Design a system that will take as input two whole numbers. If the second number is the same as or larger than the first, the system will output 'Second'; if not the output should be 'First'

a   How would this impact on the choice of logical operator?

b   Could the condition still be reversed?

6.05 Multiple IF Statements

If the previous example is expanded to provide a third output when the numbers are the same, a simple IF statement would not be sufficient to solve the problem. Problems of this nature can be solved by a series of sequential IF statements, each of which ends before the following one starts as in the example below.

```
INPUT number1                         number1 = int(input('Enter first number: '))
INPUT number2                         number2 = int(input('Enter second number: '))

IF number 2 = number1 THEN            if number2 == number1:
    OUTPUT 'Same'                         print('Same')
ENDIF

IF number 2 > number1 THEN            if number2 > number1:
    OUTPUT 'Second'                       print('Second')
ENDIF

IF number 2 < number1 THEN            if number2 < number1:
    OUTPUT 'First!'                       print('First')

ENDIF
```

Although this approach achieves the required outcome, it is inefficient. Consider the situation where both numbers are equal. The first statement would have produced the appropriate output, but even though the conditions in the following IF statements are false, the code must still execute them. The algorithm produces the required output but two IF statements have been executed unnecessarily.

6.06 Nested IF Statements

To avoid the inefficiency of multiple IF statements, it is possible to place one or more IF statements entirely within another. The second and subsequent IF statements will only be executed should the first condition prove to be false. These are known as nested IF statements.

Figure 6.04 shows how a nested IF approach could be applied to the inefficient sequence of IF statements shown in Figure 6.03. Because the second IF statement will only execute if the criteria in the first statement is False, unnecessary execution of IF statements is avoided.

```
INPUT number1                         number1 = int(input('Enter first number: '))
INPUT number2                         number2 = int(input('Enter second number: '))

IF number2 = number1 THEN             if number2 == number1:
    OUTPUT 'Same'                         print('Same')

ELSE                                  else:
    IF number2 > number1 THEN             if number2 > number1:
        OUTPUT 'Second'                   print('Second')

    ELSE                                  else:
        OUTPUT 'First'                        print('First')

    ENDIF

ENDIF
```

Notice how the colon in Python replaces the THEN in the pseudocode and that there is no need to have an ENDIF statement. When writing pseudocode in Cambridge IGCSE and O Level Computer Science papers, it is very important to include ENDIF clauses, make sure you do not forget it.

6.07 CASE Statements

CASE statements are considered an efficient alternative to multiple IF statements in circumstances where many choices depend on the value of a single variable.

Consider the situation where a user must input A, B or C. The code is required to follow different paths depending on which letter has been input. The pseudocode in Figure 6.05(a) shows the approach that would be taken using nested IF statements and Figure 6.05(b) shows a CASE statement.

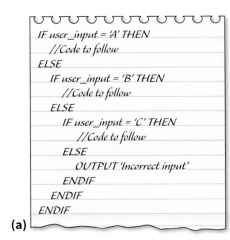

```
IF user_input = 'A' THEN
    //Code to follow
ELSE
    IF user_input = 'B' THEN
        //Code to follow
    ELSE
        IF user_input = 'C' THEN
            //Code to follow
        ELSE
            OUTPUT 'Incorrect input'
        ENDIF
    ENDIF
ENDIF
```
(a)

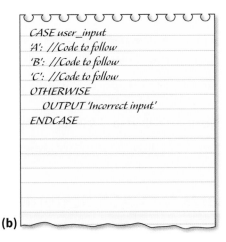

```
CASE user_input
    'A': //Code to follow
    'B': //Code to follow
    'C': //Code to follow
    OTHERWISE
        OUTPUT 'Incorrect input'
ENDCASE
```
(b)

Figure 6.03 Nested IF (a) and CASE (b) statements

Both approaches achieve the same outcome but the CASE statement is simpler to code and easier to read than the NESTED IF.

However, CASE statements are not available in Python.

6.08 Coding CASE Statements in Python

There are IF statements in Python and there is the possibility to have nested IF statements, but there is no facility to write CASE statements. There is, however, a structure that is easier to read than nested IF statements and more flexible than CASE statements available to Python programmers. Instead of a series of nested IF statements, Python programmers would use `elif` (short for ELSE IF (see section 6.08).)

43

This is how the pseudocode in Figure 6.03(a) would look in Python:

```
user_input = input('Enter A,B or C: ')

if user_input == 'A':
    # code to follow
elif user_input == 'B':
    # code to follow
elif user_input == 'C':
    # code to follow
else:
    print('Incorrect Input')
```

When trying out pseudocode CASE solutions in Python, use the `if...elif...else` construct.

Task 3

Points for discussion:

a You know that CASE statements are more efficient than a series of IF statements. Is a sequence of `elif` statements just as efficient as CASE statements?

b How are Python's `elif` statements more flexible than CASE statements?

6.09 Drawing Flowcharts for CASE Statements

CASE statements are actually the most efficient code structure we have met for choosing different outcomes based on the value of a single variable. This is because they use the value as an index and go straight to that line of code, ignoring all others. Python's `if...elif...else` construct requires each evaluation to be made until the correct one is reached (and then the rest are skipped). This is the same situation as for nested IF statements.

The flowchart for nested IF statements and the Python solution are thus the same. The flowchart for the pseudocode in Figure 6.03(a) can be seen in Figure 6.04(a). The pseudocode in Figure 6.03(b) for the solution using CASE statements is better represented by the flowchart in Figure 6.04(b).

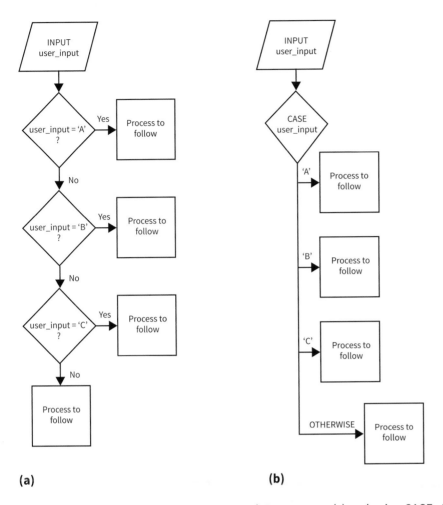

(a) **(b)**

Figure 6.04 Example flowchart using nested IF statement (a) and using CASE statements (b)

6.10 Programming Tasks

DEMO TASK

Calculator (Optional)

Create a calculator that works in this way:

1 User inputs a number.

2 User selects one of four arithmetic operators.

3 User inputs second number.

4 The appropriate output is provided.

Figure 6.05 shows the flowchart for this task and Figure 6.06 shows the pseudocode option.

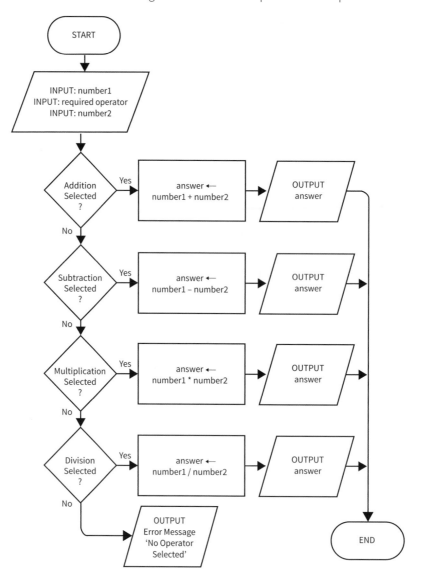

Figure 6.05 Flowchart for calculator algorithm

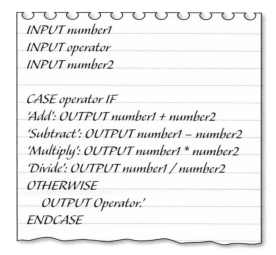

Figure 6.06 Pseudocode for calculator algorithm

The following code implements an appropriate text-based Python application:

```python
number1 = int(input('Enter First Number: '))

# Use triple speech marks to enclose multiple
# line strings to maintain formatting
print("""
Choose one of the following options:
 A for Add
 S for Subtract
 M for Multiply
 D for Divide""")
operator = input()

number2 = int(input('Enter Second Number: '))

if operator == 'A':
    print(number1+number2)
elif operator == 'S':
    print(number1-number2)
elif operator == 'M':
    print(number1*number2)
elif operator == 'D':
    print(number1/number2)
else:
    print('Incorrect Operator')
```

If coded as a GUI application, the interface might look like Figure 6.07.

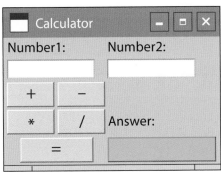

Figure 6.07 Interface for a GUI version of calculator

Producing GUI based applications is outside the syllabus.

47

TASK

Task 4 – Simple Calculator (Optional)

Write the code for a working calculator that has a GUI interface similar to that shown in Figure 6.07 that takes numbers with the Real data type rather than Integers.

Hints:
- operator will need to be a global variable.
- You will need a separate function for each operator button in your calculator. These will need to set operator to A, S, M or D as required.
- Real numbers are called Floats in Python.

Task 5 – Examination Grading System

A program is required to take as input values the number of marks a student achieved and the total number of marks available in an examination. It should output the grade obtained based on the grade boundaries in Table 6.03

Table 6.03

Grade awarded	Condition
A	Student achieves 80% or more of the marks
B	Student achieves 70% or more of the marks
C	Student achieves 60% or more of the marks
U	Student achieves less than 60% of the marks

a Produce a flow diagram for a CASE solution to this problem.

b Produce the pseudocode for a CASE solution to this problem.

c Produce a text-based Python solution to this problem that uses the `if...elif...else` construct.

Task 6 – Parcel Delivery System

A system is required to calculate the delivery cost of parcels. All parcels have a fixed charge for delivery if the parcel is 5 kg or below in weight. For local deliveries this charge is £20; for international deliveries the charge raises to £40.

The maximum weight limit for international deliveries is 5 kg; however, for local deliveries extra weight is permitted and charged at £1 for every 1 kg above that limit.

a Draw a flowchart and create a pseudocode algorithm that will identify if the parcel is local or international and then apply the appropriate weight formula to calculate the correct cost.

b Test that your algorithm works by programming and running your code in Python.

Task 7 – CO_2 Calculator

A student has been asked to create a simple carbon dioxide (CO_2) calculator. The system is intended to show the difference in emissions between petrol and diesel cars. The intended inputs are the type of fuel the car uses and whether the capacity of the engine is greater than 2 litres. The user will also input the distance travelled in the car in kilometres. The emission values in tonnes of CO_2 per 1000 kilometres are shown in Table 6.04.

Table 6.04

Fuel type	Engine size 2 litres or less	Engine size greater than 2 litres
Petrol	0.208 tonnes CO_2/1000 km	0.296 tonnes CO_2/1000 km
Diesel	0.176 tonnes CO_2/1000 km	0.236 tonnes CO_2/1000 km

a Draw a flowchart and create a pseudocode algorithm that will output the tonnes of CO_2 for the distance and type of vehicle input.

b Test that your algorithms work by programming and running the code in Python.

Task 8 – Improved Calculator (Optional)

This task can only be implemented as a GUI application.

The calculator you made earlier requires you to input two numbers into two different input text boxes. Most calculators only have one display box for both the input and output. They follow this process:

1 Input the first number in the display box.

2 Select an operator which also clears the display box and stores the first number.

3 Input the second number in the display box.

4 Select 'equals', which performs the intended operation and displays the result.

5 Select 'clear', which clears the stored values and clears the display.

   a Produce a flowchart to create a program for a calculator that has only one text box and performs the process described above.

   Hint: You may need to break this up into more than one flowchart.

   Hint: There may be an opportunity to extract some repeating code into a helper function.

   b Produce a GUI application in Python that implements your algorithm.

Producing GUI based applications is outside the syllabus.

6.11 Connecting Logical Operators

Often a single logical operator is not sufficient to define the required criteria. For example, a fire alarm system may be required to activate if it detects either the presence of smoke or a high temperature. The logical operator in this case requires two criteria, either of which being true would cause activation of the alarm.

Python, in common with many other languages, uses the logical connectors shown in Table 6.05.

Table 6.05

Operator	Description	Example in Python
AND	**All** connected operators must be True for the condition to be met.	`if student_user == True and ID_number > 600:` The condition will only be **True** where the user is a student with an ID number higher than 600. Any other type of user with an ID number > 600 will not meet the criteria because it will fail the `student_user == True` element of the condition.
OR	**Only one** of the connected operators needs to be True for the condition to be met.	`if smoke_detected == True or temperature > 70:` The condition will be True if either smoke is detected or the temperature is above 70 °C. It will also be True if both elements are met.

NOT	Used where it is easier to define the logical criteria in a negative way.	`if not input_number == 6:`
		
		The condition will be True for any number input with the exception of the number 6.
		
		Could also have been written:
		
		`if input_number != 6:`

Using AND to Provide Range Criteria

In the following code, the condition is met if the input number is greater than 10 but less than 15.

```
if num > 10 and num < 15:
    # code to execute
```

Beware of getting the wrong operator. Using or in the statement would evaluate to true for any number.

Using the AND Operator to Replace a Nested IF Statement

A nested IF statement is often used to check two conditions.

```
if student_user == True:
    if ID_number > 600:
        # code to execute
```

When the conditions are simple, the nested IF statement can be replaced by AND. The following code represents the same conditions:

```
if student_user == True and ID_number > 600:
    # code to execute
```

Using Logical Connectors

In flowcharts, we need to be able to represent logical operators. We do this with logical connectors.

The last two code snippets are shown, represented as flowcharts in Figure 6.08.

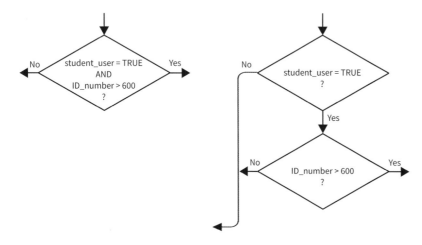

Figure 6.08 Flowchart with and without logical connectors

Task 9 – CO$_2$ Calculator Extension

If you did not already do so, rewrite the CO$_2$ emissions program from Task 7 using connected criteria.

50

The original calculator program is capable of performing only one arithmetic calculation at a time. Many calculators allow the user to enter a sequence of numbers and operators, displaying the cumulative result of the arithmetic process as the sequence is entered. An example of this process is given in Table 6.06.

Table 6.06

User input	Display	Process
43	43	
+	43	• Stores first number input • Records the addition operator selected
11	11	
*	54	• Completes the addition of the stored number with new number (43 + 11) and outputs result (54) • Records that multiplication is the latest operator selected • Stores 54 as the cumulative result
2	2	
–	108	• Completes the multiplication of the cumulative value by the new number input (54 * 2) and outputs the result (108) • Records that subtraction is the latest operator selected • Stores 108 as the cumulative result
100	100	
/	8	• Completes the subtraction of the new number from the cumulative value (108 – 100) and outputs the result (8) • Records that division is the latest operator selected • Stores 8 as the cumulative result
2	2	
=	4	• Completes the division of the cumulative value by the new number input (8 / 2) and outputs the result (4) • Records end of sequence by setting all operator indicators to False • Sets cumulative result and any interim stored numbers to 0

EXTENSION TASK

Task 10 – Cumulative Calculator (Optional)

a Produce a flowchart or pseudocode for a calculator that is capable of allowing a sequence of numbers and operators to be input. When the first operator is selected, it will store the initial value. As subsequent operators are pressed, they will complete the previous operation, storing and displaying the cumulative value. The equals button will end the sequence, display the final cumulative value and reset any variables to allow a new sequence to be input.

b Test your algorithm works by programming and running the calculator as a Python GUI application.

Producing GUI based applications is outside the syllabus.

Summary

- Selection provides methods that programmers can use to allow the algorithm to follow different paths through the code depending on the data being used at the time.

- The flowchart symbol for selection is a decision diamond. ⬦ The selection criterion is included in the symbol. The exit paths should be indicated as Yes and No or True and False.

- Multiple decisions are shown as a series of connected decisions.

- Logical operators are used to provide a range of comparative options.

- IF statements provide the ability to use complex criteria based on multiple variables or user inputs.

- A String of separate IF statements can usually be replaced by more efficient nested IFs or CASE statements.

- Nested IF statements provide the ability for additional conditions to be checked once a path has been determined by earlier conditions.

- CASE statements provide a simple method of providing multiple paths based on a single variable or user input. They are not available in Python and should be replaced with `if . . . elif . . . else`

- The ELSE statement (used with IF) and the OTHERWISE statement (used with CASE) provide a default path should none of the conditions be met.

Chapter 7:
Iteration

Learning objectives

By the end of this chapter you will understand:

- the need for iteration
- how to design and represent iteration using flowcharts and pseudocode
- how to write code that will repeat instructions a predetermined number of times
- how to write code that will repeat instructions based on user input
- how to use counters with repeated code
- the advantages and disadvantages of FOR, WHILE and REPEAT UNTIL loops.

7.01 The Need for Iteration

Many processes and algorithms will complete repetitive operations on changing data. For example, a system that is required to check that a series of 100 numbers are all above a certain value would be required to check each value against the same condition. It would be impractical to reproduce that code a hundred times; a better alternative would be to rerun the same checking algorithm a hundred times with the input value changing each time the code is repeated. Another algorithm may be required to evaluate each character in a String; a loop could be used to rerun the evaluation code for each character in the String.

7.02 Types of Iteration

Three basic forms of iteration (Table 7.01) exist in the majority of programing languages. They are known as 'loops', because they cause the program to repeatedly 'loop through' the same lines of code.

Table 7.01

Loop type	Description	When it should be used
FOR loop	Repeats a section of code a predetermined number of times	The number of iterations is known or can be calculated.
		The programmer can set the code to loop the correct number of times.
WHILE loop	Repeats a section of code while the control condition is true	The number of iterations is not known and it may be possible that the code will never be required to run.
		The condition is checked before the code is executed. If the condition is false, the code in the loop will not be executed.
REPEAT UNTIL loop	Repeats a section of code until the control condition is true	The number of iterations is not known but the code in the loop must be run at least once.
		The condition is checked after the code has been executed, so the code will run at least once.

Often, it is possible to use any of the three types when producing an algorithm; however, each type offers the programmer certain advantages. Selecting the most appropriate type of loop can help to make your code more efficient.

7.03 FOR Loops

A **FOR loop** can only be used where the number of iterations is known at the time of programming. Often this will be in a situation when the number of iterations is 'hard-coded', but it is also possible to make use of variables when identifying the number of iterations.

> **SYLLABUS CHECK**
>
> **Pseudocode:** understand and use pseudocode, using FOR . . . TO . . . NEXT loop structures.

These are also known as 'count-controlled' loops, because the number of iterations is controlled by a loop counter. It is traditional to use a variable named i (an abbreviation for the word 'index') as the control variable.

Here is the pseudocode and Python syntax for a FOR loop:

```
FOR i 1 TO 10
    //Code to execute
NEXT
```

```python
for i in range(1,11):
    # Code to execute
```

Notice how neither the pseudocode nor the Python code need to increment i within the loop; this is handled automatically by FOR loops. Do not forget, however, to add a line such as i = i + 1 to your flowcharts.

Let's look at the pseudocode first. Each individual element of the loop performs an important role in achieving the iteration as shown in Table 7.02.

Table 7.02

Element	Description
FOR	The start of the loop.
i = 1 TO 10	i is a counter variable that records the number of iterations that have been run. This is usually incremented by 1 every iteration. There is no requirement to declare the counter variable separately – it is automatically declared as part of the FOR loop. The value of the counter variable can be used within the loop to perform incremental calculations.
NEXT	The end of the iteration section.
	The value of the counter variable is incremented and the flow of the program goes back to the FOR line. The loop will evaluate to see if the counter value is still within the condition (10 in this example). If the counter has exceeded the end value, the loop will direct the flow of the program to the line of code following NEXT, if not it will rerun the loop.

Any code that is placed within the FOR loop will be repeated on each iteration. The repeated code can itself include complex processes such as selection or additional loops.

TIP

As the conditions are checked at FOR, NEXT will always pass execution of the loop back to FOR to check the conditions. It is a common misconception that once the maximum number of iterations has been reached, NEXT will exit the loop. This is not true. Consider a situation where a FOR loop is written to execute ten times. Although the loop counter may have reached 10, NEXT will still increment the counter to 11 before passing execution to FOR. The value of the loop counter will be outside the criteria and FOR will then exit the loop.

The Python code is somewhat different. Just as there are several types of loops in different languages, there are also different types of FOR loop. Python FOR loops are optimised for container variables (these feature in Chapter 11). There is no implementation of a counter FOR loop in Python. The FOR loop in Python instead iterates through a group of variables and finds out for itself how many items there are in that group. This is very powerful. However, to provide an implementation that is analogous to the pseudocode style FOR loop used in the syllabus, it requires the use of the **range()** function to generate a sequence.

range() takes three arguments:

- the Integer to start at (default = 0).

- the first Integer to exclude (required).

- the amount to increment by (default = 1).

Study the interactive sessions below to see how `range()` produces sequences of numbers. Note that the `list()` function is used to cast the sequence produced into a form that can be seen in the Python Shell. (You will learn about lists in Chapter 11.)

Create a sequence of numbers starting at 3 and ending before 10 in increments of 2:

```
>>> list(range(3, 10, 2))
[3, 5, 7, 9]
```

To create a sequence of numbers starting at 3 and ending before 10 in increments of 1:

```
>>> list(range(3, 10)) # if left out, the default increment is 1
[3, 4, 5, 6, 7, 8, 9]
```

To create a sequence of numbers starting at 0 and ending before 10 in increments of 1:

```
>>> list(range(10)) # if left out, the default start is 0
[0, 1, 2, 3, 4, 5, 6, 7, 8, 9]
```

So to produce a sequence of numbers from 1 to 10, we call range(1,11) and so

```
for i in range(1,11):
```

can be read as, 'For all items in the sequence [1, 2, 3, 4, 5, 6, 7, 8, 9, 10] loop through once and refer to the current item as `i`.'

DEMO TASK

Multiplier

A system is required to output the multiples of a given number up to a maximum of 10 multiples. For example, the multiples of 6 are 6, 12, 18, 24, 30, 36, 42, 48, 54 and 60.

Figure 7.01 shows the flowchart and pseudocode for the design of the algorithm.

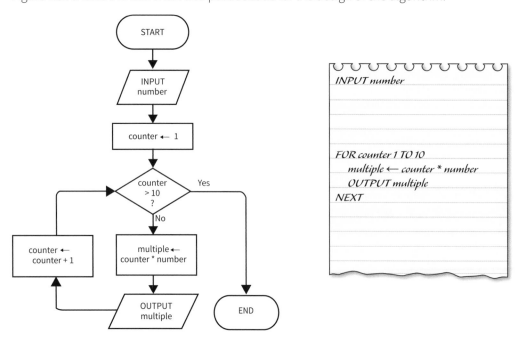

Figure 7.01 Flowchart and pseudocode for outputting multiples

Pseudocode: understand and use pseudocode for counting (e.g. Count ← Count +1).

The code for the text-based application in Figure 7.01 could be similar to the following:

```
# multiples.py

# Input the user number, cast string input to an integer
# and store in the variable number
number = int(input("Input number to multiply: "))

for counter in range(1,11):
    multiple = number * counter
    print(multiple)
```

If the user enters 4, then the output from this program would be:

```
4
8
12
16
20
24
28
32
36
40
```

The GUI application in Figure 7.02 makes use of a text box that holds multiple lines of text. The layout has been achieved without using frames. The window size and colour have been provided by using tkinter's `geometry()` and `configure()` methods. A trick has been used to provide vertical spacing above the label. Can you see how this was achieved?

Producing GUI based applications is outside the syllabus.

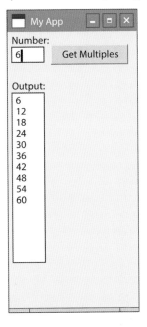

Figure 7.02 GUI application of multiplier

57

Items are added to the list box by using the code:

```
<Text box name>.insert(END, <string to add>)
```

The data to be added must be a String but as the result of the calculation is an Integer, it has to be cast with `str()` before it can be added to the text box. The code to achieve Figure 7.02 would be:

```python
# multiples-gui.py

from tkinter import *

def multiply():
    # get contents of textbox_input
    number = int(textbox_input.get())

    # clear output text box
    textbox_output.delete(0.0, END)

    # process and output result
    for counter in range(1,11):
        multiple = str(number * counter) + '\n'
        textbox_output.insert(END, multiple)

# Build the GUI
window = Tk()
window.title('My App')

# give the window a size and background colour
window.geometry('150x350')
window.configure(background='linen')

# Create the labels
input_label = Label(window, text='Number: ', bg='linen')
input_label.grid(row=0, column=0)
output_label = Label(window, text='\nOutput: ', bg='linen')
output_label.grid(row=2, column=0)

# Create text entry box for entering number
textbox_input = Entry(window, width=5)
textbox_input.grid(row=1, column=0)

# Create text box for outputting multiples
textbox_output = Text(window, height=15, width=6)
textbox_output.grid(row=3, column=0)

# Create the button
multiply_button = Button(window, text='Multiply', command=multiply)
multiply_button.grid(row=1, column=1)

window.mainloop()
```

The trick to provide the vertical space above the label was to include a line return \n before the rest of the label text.

Task 1

Extend the multiply system to include two inputs. The first input is the number to multiply, the second is the number of multiples required.

Task 2

Produce a system that accepts two numbers, a and b, and outputs a^b. For example, if a = 3 and b = 4, the output will be 81 ($3^4 = 3 \times 3 \times 3 \times 3$).

7.04 Using Loops with Advanced Arithmetic Operators

In Chapter 3, we learnt about the use of basic arithmetic operators such as add and divide. Python offers more advanced arithmetic operators.

A particular example of this is the way in which we divide numbers. It would be normal to expect the result of a division to be an exact value such as 91/24 = 3.792. But if you are dealing with data that can only be represented as Integers then a different approach might be needed.

If you had to organise transport for a group of 91 people using buses that can hold a maximum of 24 people you are more likely to want to express 91/24 in the format '3 remainder 19'. This format would allow you to identify that you would need four buses and still have seats available for another five people. The arithmetic terms for these items are 'quotient' and 'modulus' (Table 7.03) and they prove useful when producing certain mathematical algorithms.

Table 7.03

Operator	Description	Python code
Quotient	A division operation that outputs the Integer part of the result. This is also known as Integer division.	The Integer division operator is two slashes: `91//24 = 3`
Modulus	A division operation that outputs the remainder part of the result. The amount by which one number will not exactly divide into another.	The modulus operator is a percentage symbol: `91%24 = 19`

Figure 7.03 shows the flowchart and pseudocode for a solution.

Prime 1

A prime number can only be divided equally by 1 or itself. If a number can divide equally into another number, the modulus of that operation will be zero. Therefore a prime number can also be defined as a number that, when divided by all the positive Integers between 1 and itself, will not result in a modulus of zero. A system is required that uses this rule to determine if a number is a prime.

59

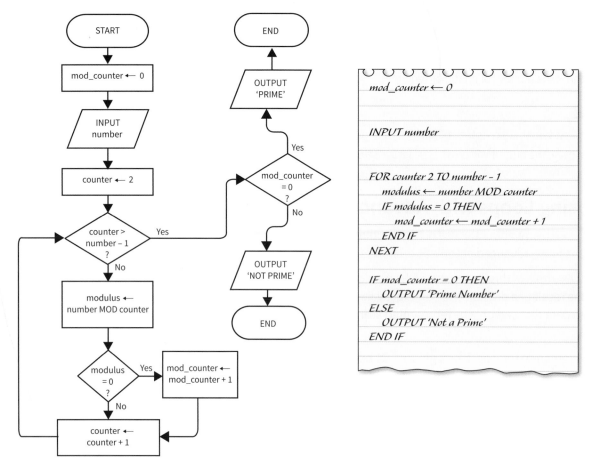

Figure 7.03 Flowchart and pseudocode for the prime algorithm

Note that in both designs, the iteration `counter` starts from 2 and ends at `number-1` to avoid the use of 1 and the number that is input occurring in the loop. These would result in a modulus of zero. To achieve the same thing when using the `range()` function in Python, we provide the arguments 2 and `number`.

TASK

Task 3 – Discussion Question

Is limiting the iterations to `number-1` the most efficient range limiter? What might be a better option?

The following is the code for a text-based Python implementation:

```python
modulus_counter = 0

number = int(input('Enter your number: '))

for counter in range(2,number):
    modulus = number % counter
    if modulus == 0:
        modulus_counter = modulus_counter + 1

if modulus_counter == 0:
    print('Prime number.')
else:
    print('Not a prime number.')
```

TASK

Task 4 (Optional)

Design a GUI version of this application giving a background colour of your choice to the window.

Producing GUI based applications is outside the syllabus.

7.05 Condition-controlled Loops

The WHILE . . . DO . . . ENDWHILE and REPEAT . . . UNTIL loop structures are controlled by a specific condition. Iterations are repeated continuously based on certain criteria. These types of loops allow iteration where the number of repetitions is unknown.

Consider the situation where one random number was constantly subtracted from another until the resultant value was less than zero. It would be impossible to determine the number of iterations required to cause the first number to be less than zero. As a result, a FOR loop would not be appropriate; another iterative method would have to be used.

While Loops

Iterations continue while the loop conditions remain true irrespective of the number of iterations this may generate. It is usual for the code within the loop to have an impact on the conditional values of the loop in such a way that the criteria will eventually become false and the loop will cease.

Because the conditions are tested at the start, it is possible that the loop will never run if the conditions are false at the outset. It is also possible to inadvertently code an infinite loop where the conditions remain true for ever.

When writing a **WHILE loop** in Python you use the following format:

```python
while counter > 0:
    # code to be iterated
    counter = counter - 1
```

This is very similar to the Cambridge IGCSE and O Level Computer Science pseudocode format:

```
WHILE counter > 0 DO
    //code to be iterated
    counter = counter – 1
ENDWHILE
```

KEY TERMS

WHILE loop: A type of iteration that will repeat a sequence of code while a set of criteria continue to be met. If the criteria are not met at the outset the loop will not run and the code within it will not be executed.

SYLLABUS CHECK

Pseudocode: understand and use pseudocode, using WHILE . . . DO . . . ENDWHILE loop structures.

Each individual element of the loop performs an important role in achieving the iteration, as shown in Table 7.04.

62

Table 7.04

Element	Description
while	The start of the loop
counter > 0	The condition that controls the loop. Each time the iteration is run, the condition is evaluated and if it remains True, the iteration will run. Once the condition is False, execution of the code is directed to the line following the loop. In counter-controlled WHILE loops, it is important that code is included within the loop to increment or decrement the counter. In a FOR loop, the counter is automatically incremented. The same facility does not apply to WHILE loops and, as a result, the programmer must include appropriate code.
end of indented code	The end of the current iteration. Execution of the program returns to `while` so the condition can be re-evaluated and further iterations actioned. Do not forget to add ENDWHILE when writing pseudocode.

TIP

Remember that WHILE loops iterate while the condition evaluates to True. It is possible to create an infinite loop rather easily:

```
>>> while True:
        print('Hello', end='')
```

It is therefore important to know how to break out of infinite loops. To do so, hold down the _CTRL_ key on your keyboard and press _C_. Try the code above yourself in an interactive session. The optional parameter end='' provided in the print() function suppresses the default line return.

In the multiplier demo task, a system was required to output the multiples of a given number up to a maximum of ten multiples. This can also be coded with a WHILE loop.

Compare the flowchart and pseudocode in Figure 7.04 with the FOR loop example in Figure 7.01.

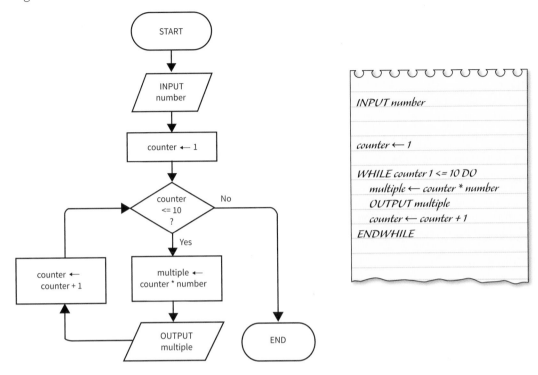

Figure 7.04 Flowchart and pseudocode for a WHILE loop

The flowcharts are nearly identical. A FOR loop always evaluates to see if the counter has reached its target and, if it has not, keeps looping. A WHILE loop can evaluate any condition and keeps looping while the condition is True. Thus, when we add a counter and evaluate against that counter, it should not be a surprise that the flowcharts are similar. The only difference is that the logical criteria are reversed in the flowchart.

The format of the WHILE loop has been followed in the pseudocode and the iterated code includes a line which increments the counter.

The following is the code for a text-based implementation:

```
number = int(input('Input number to multiply: '))

counter = 1
while counter <= 10:
    multiple = number * counter
    print(multiple)
    counter = counter + 1
```

63

Task 5

After reminding yourself how to break out of an infinite loop (see the previous Tip), try running the code above but first comment out the last line (`counter = counter + 1`). Explain the outcome of this change.

Task 6 – WHILE Loop

A WHILE loop could be used to calculate the quotient and modulus without using the built-in operators (`//` and `%`). The WHILE loop would be set to continually subtract number **b** from number **a** while **a** remains greater than or equal to **b**. When this condition is no longer true:

* the number of subtractions is equal to **a** quotient **b**
* the number remaining is equal to **a** modulus **b**.

1 Draw a flowchart and create a pseudocode algorithm that takes as input two numbers and outputs the quotient and modulus resulting from the division of the two numbers.

2 Test that your algorithm works by programming and running the code as a Python text based application.

WHILE Loops with Multiple Criteria

In the Demo Task Prime 1 in Section 7.04, the output was a message indicating if the input number was a prime or not. To achieve this, the FOR loop may have iterated many times even though the non-prime nature of the number had already been determined.

For example, any even number can be shown not to be prime just by taking the modulus division of 2, making all subsequent iterations unnecessary. A WHILE loop can provide a more efficient solution to the prime number task by looping only while no positive divisor has been tested. The loop can end at the identification of the first positive divisor or when all relevant Integer values have been tested.

> **SYLLABUS CHECK**
>
> **Problem-solving and design:** comment on the effectiveness of a given solution.

Prime 2

Construct a flowchart and pseudocode to create a WHILE loop that identifies whether a given number is a prime number or not. Then provide a Python implementation to test your solution.

The WHILE loop will need multiple criteria. In the previous algorithm a count of the number of exact divisors was maintained. In this example a Boolean value is used to indicate that an exact divisor has been identified.

Figure 7.05 shows the flowchart and pseudocode for a solution.

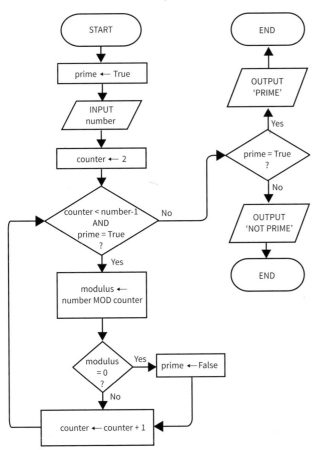

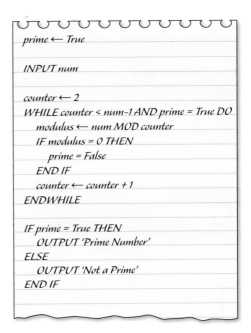

```
prime ← True

INPUT num

counter ← 2
WHILE counter < num-1 AND prime = True DO
    modulus ← num MOD counter
    IF modulus = 0 THEN
        prime = False
    END IF
    counter ← counter + 1
ENDWHILE

IF prime = True THEN
    OUTPUT 'Prime Number'
ELSE
    OUTPUT 'Not a Prime'
END IF
```

Figure 7.05 Flowchart and pseudocode for WHILE approach

The following is the code for a text-based implementation:

```
prime = True

number = int(input('Input number to test: '))

# declare counter to use with the while loop
# initialise to 2 to avoid using 1 as a divisor
counter = 2
while counter < number-1 and prime == True:
    modulus = number % counter
    if modulus == 0:
        prime = False
    counter = counter + 1

if prime == True:
    print('Your number is PRIME')
else:
    print('Your number is NOT PRIME')
```

REPEAT ... UNTIL Loops

A **REPEAT ... UNTIL loop** is very similar to a WHILE loop as iteration will continue based on the loop conditions. It is therefore also able to work in situations where the number of iterations is unknown.

KEY TERMS

REPEAT ... UNTIL loop: A type of iteration that will repeat a sequence of code until a certain condition is met.

Unlike in a WHILE loop, the test is completed at the end of the iteration so the iterated code will always run at least once.

SYLLABUS CHECK

Pseudocode: understand and use pseudocode, using REPEAT ... UNTIL loop structures.

There is no REPEAT ... UNTIL loop in Python, but your pseudocode can be implemented in Python by creating an infinite loop and then using **break** after testing at the end of the loop:

```
while True:
    # Code for iteration
    counter = counter + 1
    if counter > 10:
        break
```

The individual elements of the code perform an important role in the iteration as shown in Table 7.05.

Table 7.05

Element	Description
`while True`	The start of the loop. By replacing the normal condition that is required to evaluate to **True** with **True**, we ensure that this loop will continue forever.
	At every iteration, the execution of the program will be passed to the **while True** command. Because the loop starts before any conditions are checked, the iteration will always run at least once.
`break`	Stop looping.
`counter > 10`	The condition for the loop.
	Each time the iteration is run, the condition is evaluated. If it remains **False**, the execution is directed to **while True** and the iteration will run again. Once the condition is **True,** the execution of the code is directed to whatever code follows the loop.
	It is possible to use the logical operators (**and, or** and **not**) to structure multiple conditions. Counter-based conditions require the counter to incremented by the code contained within the loop.

TIP

Because the check is made at the end of the sequence of code, the loop will always run at least once.

Prime 3

Formulate an algorithm to calculate if a number is prime using a REPEAT . . . UNTIL loop.

The flowchart and pseudocode for the REPEAT . . . UNTIL loop are shown in Figure 7.06. If you compare these with the WHILE approach in Figure 7.05, you will be able to identify the differences in approach. The decision criteria are checked at different stages during the process, the WHILE at the outset of the loop and the REPEAT . . . UNTIL at the end. The loop decision for the WHILE is based on the criteria being True and the REPEAT . . . UNTIL loops if the criteria are False.

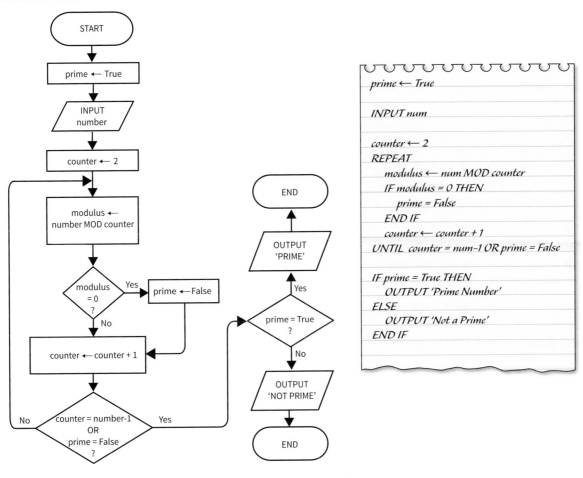

Figure 7.06 Flowchart and pseudocode for REPEAT . . . UNTIL approach

Task 7

Using the flowchart and pseudocode in Figure 7.06, produce a text-based Python implementation.

WHILE and UNTIL Criteria

When considering the criteria for a WHILE or REPEAT ... UNTIL loop, it is important to remember that the logic for each loop is defined as the opposite of the other. For example, if the criteria was based on a Boolean value, the condition would be as shown in Table 7.06.

Table 7.06

Criteria	When Boolean = False	When Boolean = True

WHILE Boolean = False DO
 	
ENDWHILE
	Continues to iterate because the Boolean is False.	Ends iteration because the Boolean is not False.

REPEAT UNTIL Boolean = True	Continues to iterate because the Boolean is not True.	Ends iteration because the Boolean is True.

7.06 WHILE and REPEAT ... UNTIL Loops Based on User Input

As both WHILE and REPEAT ... UNTIL loops are capable of iterating an unknown number of times, they are able to work in an environment where a user will input a sequence of data items and indicate the end of the sequence by inputting a specific item. Often, the data items will be a series of positive numbers and the input that will end the series is a negative number.

For example, a student is completing an experiment in which they record the height and gender of all the students who they meet in a certain time period. They are asked to indicate the end of the input process by entering a negative value for height. The program will record the average height for each gender and the total number of records entered.

In this scenario, the input would be placed within either a WHILE or a REPEAT ... UNTIL loop with the loop condition being based on the height input value. The algorithm to maintain the total number of records entered and the height averages would iterate in the loop. The output of the system would most likely be programmed to display only when the loop had ended.

In a GUI event-driven application, it is difficult to recreate this type of scenario because of its event-driven nature which makes the inclusion of input within a loop impossible. However, text-based programs can be used to show how these types of program can be written and executed.

TIP

When using iteration based on user input, it is crucial that the input is included within the loop. A common error is to include a single input outside the loop:

```
INPUT number
WHILE number > 6 DO
    OUTPUT number
ENDWHILE
```

Consider the situation if the user input the number 10. The loop will continually check against the value of 10 and run an infinite number of times. Again, an infinite loop is produced.

SYLLABUS CHECK

Pseudocode: understand and use pseudocode for totalling (e.g. Sum ← Sum + Number).

Summing User Input

A system is required which will allow a user to input a series of positive numbers indicating the end of the sequence by inputting a value of –1. The system will output the sum of the positive numbers input.

The flowchart in Figure 7.07 does not indicate either a WHILE or REPEAT . . . UNTIL loop – it simply includes the criteria in the loop.

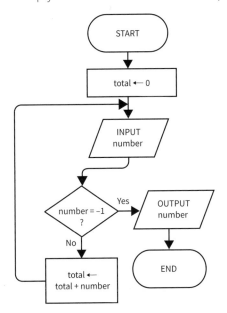

Figure 7.07 Flowchart for input loop

The different approaches can be seen in the pseudocode.

The WHILE loop in Figure 7.08(a) requires the first number to be input outside the loop to provide a value to check.

The REPEAT . . . UNTIL loop in Figure 7.08(b) will have included the input of –1 in `total` as the conditions are not checked until after the processing in the loop has been completed. Consequently, the total has to be recalculated after the loop.

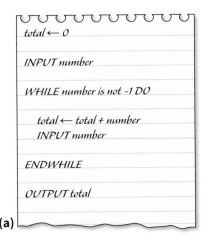

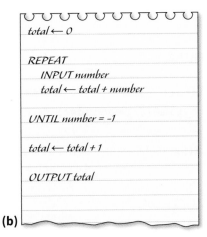

(a)

(b)

Figure 7.08 Pseudocode for WHILE and REPEAT . . . UNTIL

Task 8

a Using the pseudocode in Figure 7.08(a), produce a text-based Python WHILE loop implementation.

b Using the pseudocode in Figure 7.08(b), produce a text-based Python REPEAT . . . UNTIL loop implementation.

Task 9

The algorithms in this chapter for identifying if a number is a prime are far from perfect. It is possible to come up with far superior algorithms. You could have a competition with your fellow students to see who can produce the fastest algorithm by adding a timer to your code.

To do this you need to import Python's **time** module, get a timestamp after the user has supplied input and then, after displaying the result, collect another timestamp and use this to calculate the elapsed time.

The WHILE loop program is shown below with the timing code added:

```
# Import time module to allow testing of efficiency
from time import *

prime = True

number = int(input('Input number to test: '))

# Grab start time
start_time=time()

counter = 2
while counter < number and prime == True:
    modulus = number % counter
    if modulus == 0:
        prime = False
    counter = counter + 1

if prime == True:
    print('Your number is PRIME')
else:
    print('Your number is NOT PRIME')

# Print out current time minus start_time
print('This took', (time()-start_time), 'seconds')
```

To be fair, you will need to ensure you supply a large prime number so that your algorithms are forced to go through all their tests. You will also need to test your algorithms on the same computer.

(982451653 is a suitable large prime and 982451649 is not.)

Summary

- Iteration provides methods that programmers can use to loop through sequences of code multiple times.

- There are three main types of iteration: FOR . . . TO . . . NEXT, WHILE . . . DO . . . ENDWHILE and REPEAT . . . UNTIL loops.

- Flowcharts symbolise loops through the use of a decision with a flow line looping back to an earlier element of the diagram. The decision contains the criteria on which the iteration is based.

- A FOR . . . TO . . . NEXT loop is used where the number of iterations is known at the outset.

- Condition-controlled loop structures, such as WHILE . . . DO . . . ENDWHILE or REPEAT . . . UNTIL, are used where the number of iterations is unknown.

- WHILE . . . DO . . . ENDWHILE structures check the loop conditions at the outset of the loop. If the conditions are False, the loop will never run.

- REPEAT . . . UNTIL structures check the loop conditions at the end of the first iteration. Consequently, the loop will always run at least once.

- WHILE . . . DO . . . ENDWHILE loops continue to iterate while the condition equates to True.

- REPEAT . . . UNTIL loops continue iterating while the condition equates to False.

- To implement a counting FOR loop in Python, the `range()` function is used.

71

Chapter 8:
Designing Algorithms

Learning objectives

By the end of this chapter you will understand:

- that systems are made up of subsystems, which may in turn be made up of further subsystems
- how to apply top-down design and structure diagrams to simplify a complex system
- how to combine the constructs of sequence, selection and iteration to design complex systems
- how to produce effective and efficient solutions to complex tasks.

8.01 The Approach

When designing algorithms, you will be making use of computational thinking. This requires the ability to analyse a scenario-based task, identify the individual elements of the task and use programming concepts to create an appropriate algorithm. Often more than one approach to a given scenario would produce a working solution, which makes this process exciting. Identifying and designing an efficient solution to a problem is at the heart of computational thinking.

8.02 Top-down Design

Top-down design is an approach to structured programming where the problem is defined in simple steps or tasks. Each of these tasks may be split into a number of smaller subtasks. The process is complete once the problem has been broken down sufficiently to allow it to be understood and programmed. This process is also known as 'step-wise refinement'.

The main advantage of designing in this way is that the final process will be well structured and easier to understand. It can increase the speed of development as different subtasks can be given to individual members of a programming team. This design approach also helps when debugging or modifying as changes can be made to individual subtasks without necessarily having to change the overall program.

This approach is effective in solving large, real-world problems as well as the type of scenario-based questions you may meet during an examination.

8.03 Structure Diagrams

One tool available to programmers when trying to design a solution to a more complex system is the Structure Diagram. Using top-down design principles, the aim is to decompose the system into smaller and smaller problems until no further decomposition can take place. At this point the programmer starts to develop algorithms for each subproblem in the usual way, using flowcharts or pseudocode.

A school requires a system that will check if students are present in lessons and report to parents any absence. The teacher will record if students are in the lesson and then transfer the record to the school administration team. They will contact parents if students are absent. The process of reporting to parents can be done either by telephone or email.

One possible strategy is to consider the situation in terms of the steps of a computer model:

Input → Storage → Process → Output.

We could start the design by considering the main elements of the required system:

- The main input will be the record of the students' presence.

- To store this some form of list could be used.

- The process will involve the following sequence of steps:

  1 recording the presence of every student who attends the lesson (this will be an iterative process).

  2 passing the list to the administration team who will contact parents.

Figure 8.01 shows the initial structure diagram for this system.

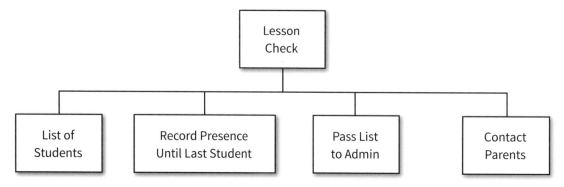

Figure 8.01 Initial structure diagram

The next step is to consider if any of the tasks could be broken down into subtasks. Creating the 'List of Students' is a high-level task that could be broken down into subtasks. Contacting parents can be done by telephone or email and will therefore need subtasks. Figure 8.02 shows the amended structure diagram with these subtasks.

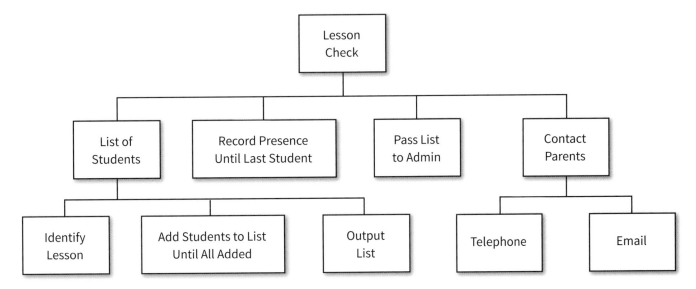

Figure 8.02 Structure diagram showing subtasks

The diagram may not yet be complete. The process 'Identify Lesson' could be broken into further subtasks. What inputs would be needed? Where is the data about which students attend the lesson stored? How will the system access those records? This and other tasks would require consideration if this was a real-life scenario.

8.04 Design Steps

As suggested above, splitting the overall task into subtasks can be done following the Input → Storage → Process → Output computer model. This will be required when preparing the pre-release material for Paper 2 (see Chapter 12). When designing an algorithm for a subtask, it is recommended that a slight adaption is made to the process:

1 Identify the inputs and outputs that are involved in the scenario. At this stage, it is worth identifying any global variables that will be required.

2 For each input, identify if the task requires this input to be repeated. This will mean some form of iteration is needed. Identify the most appropriate loop to use.

3 For each output, identify the required calculation or recording process required to produce the output value.

   a Does the process involve any decision making? This could mean use of an IF statement.

   b Does the process involve repeated calculation? This could mean some form of iteration.

4 Consider the sequence in which the various processes need to be completed:

   • Check that inputs or processes that need to be iterated are within the loop.

   • Check that single inputs and outputs are outside the loop.

   • Check any iteration repeats as expected.

   • Check you have defined and initialised the variables or constants that are to be used.

Considering the inputs and outputs at the start will help you to consider the aim of the system. If you don't consider the required outputs early in the design stage, how can you define the process required to produce the outputs?

Although considered at the outset, variables can be finalised as a last step to making sure nothing has been missed.

TIP

When programming, the IDE will alert you to incorrect statements and missing variables. When designing in pseudocode, this support is not available. Always check that you have initialised all global variables correctly and that program statements are complete.

SYLLABUS CHECK

Problem solving and design: produce an algorithm for a given scenario in the form of a flowchart or pseudocode.

DEMO TASK

Design: Known Quantity of Inputs

A user will input 100 positive numbers into a system. The system will output the highest number and the sum of the numbers input. Design an appropriate algorithm.

76

Figure 8.03 outlines the computational thinking process for designing the algorithm using the steps described above.

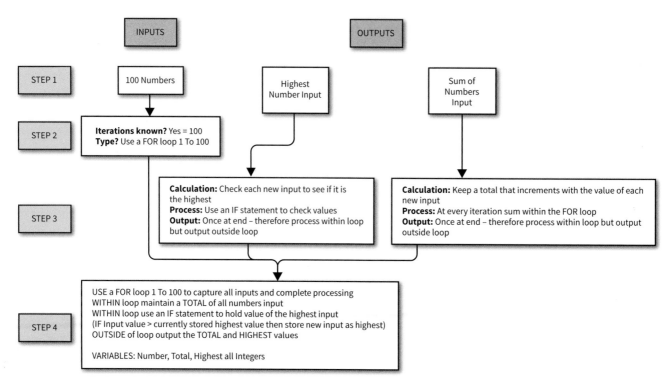

Figure 8.03 The steps in computational thinking

The structure diagram in Figure 8.04 shows the design of the process.

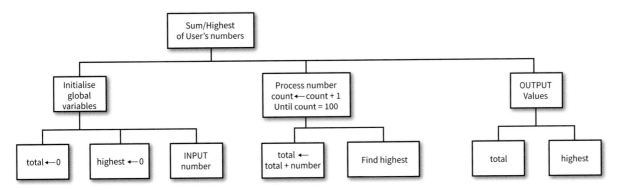

Figure 8.04 Structure diagram

The resultant flowchart and pseudocode are shown in Figure 8.05.

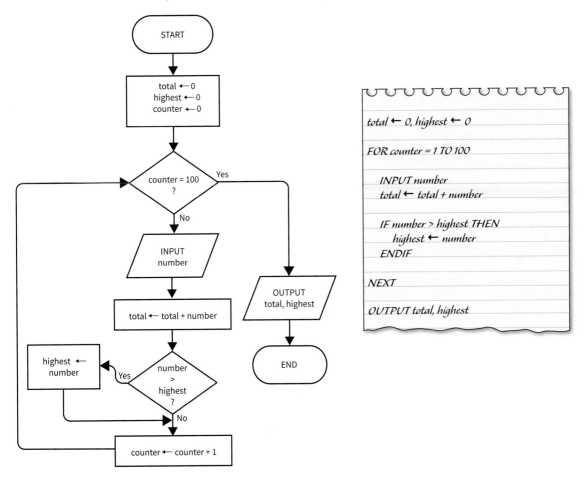

Figure 8.05 Flowchart and pseudocode approach

Task 1 – Discussion Question

This is not the only acceptable solution. Identify two other ways this algorithm could have been written.

Task 2 – Design: Unknown Quantity of Inputs

A user is required to input the population of a number of local cities. They will indicate the end of the input sequence by inputting a negative value. The system will output the average population of all the cities.

TIP

To check that your solution works as intended it should be tested. See Chapter 10 to discover how this can be achieved.

8.05 The complete design process

When presented with a complex problem, any or all of the following processes might be needed to create a finished solution:

- Decomposition – using **top-down design** and **structured diagrams**

- Standard methods of solution – using **flow charts** and **pseudocode** initially and then examining the algorithm to see if it could be **simplified**, or made more **efficient** by employing loops or subroutines

- Check input data – This is called **validating** user input (see Chapter 9)

- Testing – thorough **testing** needs to then take place (see Chapter 10)

Simplifying algorithms makes for more reliable and maintainable solutions. Efficient algorithms use loops and functions to collect repetitive input and processing. An efficient algorithm will combine the collection of multiple processes in one loop rather than in separate loops wherever possible.

You are expected to be able to design effective solutions and comment on the effectiveness of algorithms presented to you. Remember to check whether the solution could be simplified further or made more efficient as well as whether it handles all your test data (Chapter 10), and that all input is effectively validated (Chapter 9). The efficiency of different solutions is examined in more depth in Chapter 7 where the use of different kinds of loops is compared, and again in Chapter 12 where advice is given on how to prepare for the pre-release tasks for Paper 2. Preparing for the pre-release tasks will involve most, if not all, of the processes above.

SYLLABUS CHECK

Explain standard methods of solution.
Comment on the effectiveness of a given solution.

Standard methods of solution: The two main standard methods of solution used throughout this book are flowcharts and pseudocode. Other standard methods of solution include, top-down design, structure diagrams, simplification, efficiency analysis, validation and testing.

8.06 Design Challenges

The following is a series of examination-style tasks.

For each task, design an appropriate algorithm using a flowchart and pseudocode. Examples of working algorithms are included in Chapter 14, but remember these are not the only possible solutions.

Task 3

A student is completing a mathematical probability study. They are required to throw a standard six-sided dice 100 times. They will input the number shown at each throw into a system. The system will output the number of times the dice shows a six and the average value of all the throws.

Task 4

The student completing the mathematical probability study in Task 3 decides to extend the study to include two standard six-sided dice. The student will throw both dice simultaneously, inputting both numbers shown at each throw into a system. The system will record the number of 'doubles' (throws that result in both dice showing the same number). The process will end when 100 doubles have been recorded, at which time the system will output the percentage of total throws that resulted in a double.

Task 5

A user inputs into a system a sequence of positive numbers. They indicate the end of the sequence by inputting the value –1. The system will output the highest and lowest numbers input.

Task 6

A user has been asked to investigate the numbers of students that are studying at schools in a geographical region. The user is required to input the name of the school and the number of its students for all 200 schools in the region. The system will output the name of the school with the highest number of students and the name of the school with the lowest number of students.

Task 7

A scientist is using a temperature sensor to record the exothermic reaction caused when two chemicals are mixed. Both chemicals start at the same temperature (which is recorded in the system). Once every minute, the sensor sends the temperature of the combined chemicals to the system. The system will continue to record the temperature values as long as the temperature remains above the initial start temperature. The expected output is the length of time in minutes the reaction takes to return to the initial value. It should also show the highest temperature reached and the time, in minutes from the start of the experiment, that this temperature was reached.

Summary

- Systems are made up of subsystems, which may in turn be made up of further subsystems.

- Top-down design is a method of simplifying the main system into its subsystems until the whole is sufficiently defined to allow it to be understood and programmed.

- Structure diagrams are a diagrammatical method of expressing a system as a series of subsystems

- When designing solutions for a given problem adopting an Input → Storage → Process → Output approach can help to design an effective solution.

- Standard methods of solution – flowcharts, pseudocode, top-down design, structure diagrams, simplification, efficiency analysis, validation and testing – are used when designing programmed systems.

- Effective solutions are ones that cannot be further simplified, are efficient, pass a testing regime and have effective validation of input.

Chapter 9:
Checking Inputs

Learning objectives

By the end of this chapter you will understand:

- the need for accuracy in inputs
- how to design validation routines using flowcharts or pseudocode
- the role and use of a range of validation techniques:
  - presence check
  - range check
  - length check
  - type check
  - format check
  - check digit
- how to program validation into your algorithms.

9.01 The Need for Accuracy

Organisations rely on the accuracy of their data when making decisions. Inaccurate data can compromise the validity of those decisions possibly with devastating results. Consider the situation of doctors receiving inaccurate medical data about patients or firefighters being given inaccurate data about wind speed and direction. The largest source of inaccuracies is during the data entry process. It is important that systems are designed to help increase the accuracy of data entry.

9.02 Validation

Validation is the process of programming a system to automatically check that data that falls outside a set of specified criteria is recognised as invalid. While validation cannot guarantee that data entered is accurate, it does ensure that it is reasonable. Systems should also filter out obvious mistakes. For example, if a system was recording the height of students, it would be reasonable to expect that they were all under 3 metres tall. Programming the system to reject data entries above 3 metres would help to remove obvious errors. However if a student's height was measured at 1.4 metres, but inaccurately entered as 1.04, the system would still accept the value because it meets the validation criteria.

> **SYLLABUS CHECK**
>
> **Problem-solving and design:** understand the need for validation checks to be made on input data.

> **TIP**
> Validation does not make data input accurate – this is a common misconception.

Table 9.01 shows different types of validation checks.

Table 9.01

Validation type	Description	Example
Presence check	Checks that required data has been input. The system will reject groups of data where required fields have been left blank. This is often used with data collection forms.	Online order where 'Email Address' must be provided.
Range check	Checks data falls within a reasonable range. Data outside the expected range is rejected. It is possible to have data where the range limit is only applicable to one extreme. For example, the volume of a vessel cannot be zero but may not have an upper limit. This is known as a 'limit check'.	Age must be between 0 and 130 inclusive. Day of the month must be between 1 and 31 inclusive. Percentage score in an exam must be between 0 and 100 inclusive.
Length check	Checks that data entered is of a reasonable length. Data items that have a length outside the expected values are rejected. Normally used with text-based inputs.	Surname must be between 1 and 25, inclusive, characters long. A password must have more than 6 characters.
Type check	Checks that a data item is of a particular data type. It will reject any input that is of a different type.	Stock items must be entered as an Integer. Age will be numeric (e.g. it will not accept 'over 21').

Validation type	Description	Example
Format check	Checks that a data item matches a predetermined pattern and that the individual elements of the data item have particular values or data types.	Date of birth will be in the format dd/mm/yyyy. Mobile telephone number will be in the format NNNNN NNNNNN where N is a digit.
Check digit	Checks that a numerical data item has been entered accurately. Extra digit(s) are added to the number based on a calculation that can be repeated, enabling the number to be checked by repeating the calculation and comparing the calculated check digit with the value entered.	A barcode includes a check digit. ISBNs (book numbers) include a check digit.

9.03 Verification

Verification confirms the integrity of data as it is input into the system or when it is transferred between different parts of a system. Data integrity refers to the correctness of data during and after processing. Although the format of the data may be changed by processing, if data integrity has been maintained the data will remain a true and accurate representation of the original. Copying data should clearly not change the data values.

Most verification techniques are undertaken by the person inputting the data and involve the checking of the data input into the system against the original. One form of verification that you could program is 'double entry' verification. The data item is entered twice, often by different operators; the system compares the input values and identifies any differences.

9.04 Programming Validation into Your Systems

Running code without passing the correct values to the variables will cause a program to crash or provide unexpected results. Run any of your programs without inputting the required numeric values and you will receive an error message. This is illustrated in the following interactive session:

```
INTERACTIVE SESSION

>>> a = '1'
>>> b = 2
>>> c = a + b
Traceback (most recent call last):
  File "<pyshell#4>", line 1, in <module>
    c=a+b
TypeError: Can't convert 'int' object to str implicitly
>>>
```

This is important when getting user input of numbers in Python as the `input()` function always returns String data types. Python will not cast a String to a number without being explicitly asked to. Should this happen in a published program, the system would crash unexpectedly.

To avoid this type of error, validation should first try to cast the user input to a number with either `int()` or `float()`. If this process fails, the data entered should be rejected as a number of the correct sort was not entered.

Presence Check Validation

Code is required to check whether the user has input a value into a required field. If the data item is present, it will pass the presence check. This is no guarantee that the data item is in an acceptable format and additional validation may be required.

Figure 9.01 shows a flowchart for a simple presence check on user input in which a textual value is required.

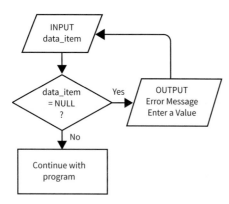

Figure 9.01 Presence check flowchart

In text-based programs, a WHILE loop can be used to check the presence of the input. If the data is missing, then the user can be prompted again to enter the required data.

```python
data_item = input('Insert text value: ')

while data_item == '':
    print('Please input text value.')


# program continues
```

In GUI applications, the execution of code is triggered by an event such as a button press. The trigger cannot be controlled from within a WHILE loop in the same way. A different approach is therefore needed.

For comparison with the text-based code above, the following code provides a GUI implementation. A message is displayed in a label widget that previously held an empty String and so was not visible:

```python
def button_click():

    if text_box.get() == '':
        my_label.config(text='Enter text here:')
    else:
        # program continues with for example:
        user_input = text_box.get()
```

> Producing GUI based applications is outside the syllabus.

Note how this does not use a WHILE loop because the text box entry only has to be processed if the button is pressed. The tkinter `mainloop()` method, however, is running in its own loop that constantly checks for all events, including button presses.

Range Check Validation

Figure 9.02 shows a flowchart and pseudocode for a range check used to ensure the day of the month entered by a user is in the range 1 to 31. The code uses a WHILE loop that checks the data against the required criteria. If the data input is acceptable, the system will continue to run. If not, the system will output an error message to the user.

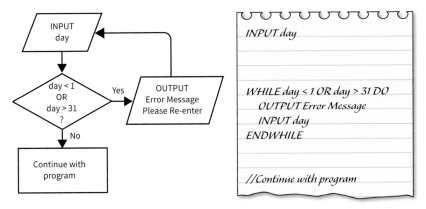

Figure 9.02 Flowchart and pseudocode for range check

```
day = int(input('Enter the day of the month: '))

while day < 1 or day > 31:
    day = int(input('Enter a value between 1 and 31: '))

# Program continues
```

TIP

WHILE loops check criteria before running. The criteria are defined to identify inputs outside the required range. If an acceptable value is input, the loop never runs and the program continues. If an input is outside the expected range, the loop continues to iterate. This effectively halts the program until an acceptable value is input.

Length Check Validation

Figure 9.03 shows a flowchart and the pseudocode for a length check to ensure that a password consists of six or more characters. The code needs to calculate the length of the password. It then follows a similar process to a range check using a WHILE loop to check the input against the required criteria. If the data input is acceptable, the system will continue to run; if not, the system will output an error message to the user.

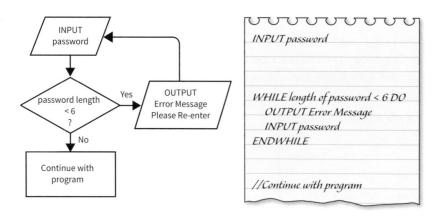

Figure 9.03 Flowchart and pseudocode for length check

```python
password = input('Enter password: ')

while len(password) < 6:
    password = input('Your password must have 6 or more characters: ')

# Program continues
```

TIP

Note the use of the `len()` function to return the number of characters in a String.

Type Check Validation

Figure 9.04 shows a flowchart and pseudocode for a type check. This ensures that a number is entered as an Integer. The code will need to identify the data type. It then uses a WHILE loop to check the input against the required criteria. If the data input is acceptable, the system will continue to run; if not, the system will output an error message to the user.

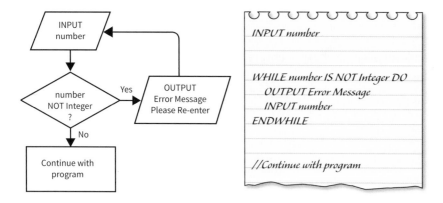

Figure 9.04 Flowchart and pseudocode for type check

While the pseudocode solution for type check validation is reasonably straightforward, the code approach is more complex. Python's `input()` function returns a String, so we would normally cast this to an Integer with the `int()` function. However, if the input is not an

Integer then the program will crash. What we want to do is evaluate the form of the input String. There is a function called **eval()** that we can use that does just this and then returns the appropriate type. Look at how this works in this interactive session:

```
INTERACTIVE SESSION

>>> number = input('Enter number: ')
Enter number: 2.1
>>> type(number)
<class 'str'>
>>> number = eval(number)
>>> type(number)
<class 'float'>
>>>
```

So one coded solution would be:

```
number = input('Please input a number: ')

while type(eval(number)) is not int:
    number = input('Not an integer. Please enter an integer: ')

# Program continues
```

A more advanced approach is to have a go at casting to an Integer and then use Python's built in **try...except** error handling code like this:

```
number = input('Please input a number: ')

while True:
    try:
        int(number)
        break
    except:
        number = input('Not an integer. Please enter an integer: ')

# Program continues
```

Notice how this solution puts the exception handling code in an infinite loop and then uses the **break** keyword to exit when the required conditions are met.

Format Check Validation

Figure 9.05 shows a flowchart and pseudocode for a format check to ensure that a date is in the format dd/mm/yyyy. The code will be required to check each element of the user input to ensure it matches a predetermined pattern. If the date matches the pattern, the system will continue to run; if not, the system will output an error message to the user.

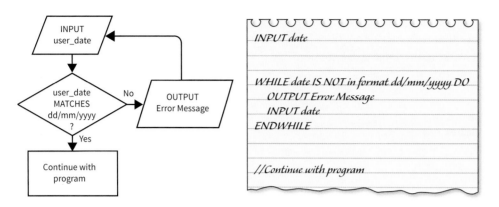

Figure 9.05 Flowchart and pseudocode for format check

As you might expect, Python has built-in libraries for validating a number of data types. As we are trying to ensure the integrity of this data, it is best, whenever possible, to use tried and tested methods. As this might well be a common requirement in a program, it might be best to implement the validation in a function and then call it. The code below imports the `datetime` methods from the `datetime` library and then implements the algorithm in the `validate _ date()` function. A call for user input and the use of the function have been added to show how to use this function whenever a user is required to input a date.

```
from datetime import datetime

def validate_date(d):
    while True:
        try:
            return datetime.strptime(d, '%d/%m/%Y')
        except:
            d = input('Date must be in the format dd/mm/yyyy: ')

date = input('Please enter a date: ')
date = validate_date(date)


# Program continues
```

The `validate _ date()` function tries to return a Python date data type that is now much safer and more flexible for the programmer to use than the initial String. If the `strptime()` function does not get passed a String in the pattern specified, an exception is thrown and the user is asked to try again. The `return` keyword is the equivalent of a `break` command but also returns a value. There are many patterns that can be asked for: `'%d/%m/%Y'` matches the requested format. More information can be found at: https://docs.python.org/3.5/library/datetime.html#strftime-strptime-behavior.

Check Digit Validation

Figure 9.06 shows a flowchart and pseudocode for an ISBN-13 check digit validation. In ISBN-13 validation, the 13th digit is removed as this is the check digit. All the other numbers are assigned a 1 or 3, alternating from 1. These numbers are used as multipliers for their corresponding digits. All the products are added together, the remainder after dividing this by 10 is found. The remainder is then subtracted from 10. This should match the check digit if the ISBN number is correct.

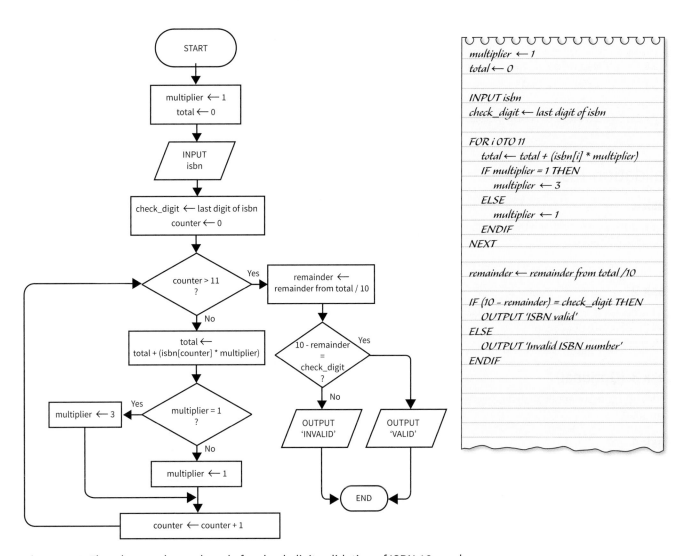

Figure 9.06 Flowchart and pseudocode for check digit validation of ISBN-13 numbers

The ISBN number, taken as input, is a pseudo-number. This is input as a string and each digit is accessed by the string index (starting from zero). This is discussed further in Chapter 11.

```
multiplier = 1
total = 0

# Input an ISBN-13 number as a string
isbn = input('Input an ISBN-13 number with no spaces: ')

# Obtain the 13th digit (all characters in string are numbered from zero)
check_digit = int(isbn[12])

# Iterate through the first 12 digits of the ISBN number
for i in range(12):
    total = total + (int(isbn[i]) * multiplier)
    if multiplier == 1:
        multiplier = 3
    else:
        multiplier = 1
```

```
remainder = total % 10

if (10 - remainder) == check_digit:
    print('ISBN valid')
else:
    print('Invalid ISBN number')
```

Validation Tasks

Task 1

a Produce a flowchart and the pseudocode for a system that will only accept positive numbers.

b Code a text-based application for this algorithm.

Task 2

a Produce a flowchart and the pseudocode for a system that will only accept positive numbers less than 1000.

b Code a text-based application for this algorithm.

Task 3 (Optional)

Code a Python GUI application for a system that will only accept positive numbers less than 1000.

Task 4

a Produce a flowchart and the pseudocode for a system that will check that users have input a password that is longer than six characters.

b Code a program for this algorithm.

Task 5

Program a function that will validate a user number and password from the user. All inputs must be validated against the following criteria:

- The user number must be a whole number in the range 1000 to 1500.

- The password must contain at least five characters.

The function will be passed the parameters of username and password and will return a Boolean value to indicate if the inputs match the validation criteria.

Task 6

Produce a flowchart and pseudocode for a system that makes use of the function in Task 5. If the validation is completed successfully the system will output 'Welcome'. If the validation check is failed twice the system will output 'Locked Out' and exit the program.

Hint: There are two ways of exiting a program in Python before reaching the end. First, you can wrap your main program in its own function such as `main()` and then call it at the end of your script – when you want to exit `main()` you use the keyword `break`. The second method is to import the `sys` module and then call `sys.exit()`.

Producing GUI based applications is outside the syllabus.

Summary

- Accuracy of data entry is an important consideration in system design. Inaccurate data can lead to inaccurate outputs.

- Validation is a technique in which the system checks data input against a set of predetermined rules.

- Validation can identify obvious errors by detecting data that fails to meet the validation rules.

- Validation is able to ensure that data input is reasonable but cannot guarantee data accuracy.

- Six main forms of validation are used to check data as it is input:
  - presence checks ensure that data has been input
  - range checks ensure that data falls within a predetermined range of values
  - length checks ensure that data inputs contain a predetermined number of characters
  - type checks ensure that data input is of a certain data type
  - format checks ensure that data input meets a predetermined format, such as dd/mm/yyyy
  - check digits are calculated from numerical data such as a barcode and added to the end of the data.

- Verification checks the integrity of data when it is entered into the system. This is often completed by the individual inputting the data.

- Two common methods of verification are:
  - checking the input data against the original document or record
  - double entry in which the data is entered twice and the entries compared to identify differences.

Chapter 10:
Testing

Learning objectives

By the end of this chapter you will understand:

- the importance of testing systems
- how to identify logical, syntax and runtime errors
- how to dry run algorithms using trace tables
- how to identify appropriate valid, invalid and boundary data when testing systems.

10.01 Why Test Systems?

In common with many products, it is important to make sure systems work as expected before they are released to the final user. The complexity and critical nature of the system will determine the extent of the testing to be completed. The computerised air traffic control system at an airport is more critical than a smartphone game and, therefore, will have undergone extensive testing – failure could be catastrophic.

There are several notable examples of disasters caused by poor testing. The destruction of the unmanned Ariane 5 space rocket due to the failure of untested code sequences is one of the most costly: The financial implications measured in billions of dollars. An article published in the *New York Times* magazine in December 1996 has more information about it and can be found at http://www.around.com/ariane.html.

10.02 When to Test

Testing can be broken into two distinct areas.

Alpha Testing

This is completed during the programming of a system to check that the individual code sequences work as expected before they are combined to make the complete system. Testing during the programming stage can also be completed to help trace the source of unexpected outcomes.

Beta Testing

Formal testing that takes place once the system has been completed to ensure that the whole system meets expectations.

10.03 Debugging

Debugging is the process of detecting faults that cause errors in a program. This can be achieved by observing error messages produced by the IDE or by investigating unexpected results. The types of error that can occur are divided into three groups.

Logical Errors

Logical errors are errors in the design of the program that allow it to run but produce unexpected results. They can result from the use of an incorrect formula or the incorrect use of control structures such as IF statements or loops. Examples include IF statements with incorrect conditions or loops that iterate the wrong number of times. Logical errors are also caused by implementing an incorrect sequence of statements, such as performing a calculation before assigning values to the variables.

Logical errors usually do not produce error messages. The problem is with the logic of the code not the execution of the code.

Syntax Errors

Syntax errors are errors in the use of the programming language such as incorrect punctuation or misspelt variables and control words. Examples include IF statements with missing colons or incorrect use of assignment. The IDE will usually generate error messages indicating the reason for the error.

93

Runtime Errors

Runtime errors are errors that are only identified during the execution of the program. They can result from mismatched data types, overflow or divide-by-zero operations.

Data type errors include:

- passing String data to an Integer variable, which will probably cause the system to crash.

- passing Real data to an Integer variable; the variable will round the input data to the nearest whole number – the system will execute the code but produce unexpected results.

Overflow errors occur when the data passed to a variable is too large to be held by the data type selected. In the theory element of the syllabus, you will have used this term to describe a situation where a nine-bit binary number is stored in an eight-bit byte. This can often result from calculations during the execution of a program. For example, in some programming languages the data type Short can be used to hold numbers between -32 767 and +32 767. If a variable of this data type was assigned the result of the square of any number greater than 182, it would produce an overflow error. As Python is a loosely typed language, it works behind the scenes to try and avoid many of these number type problems.

In mathematics, it is not possible to divide by zero because any number can be divided by zero an infinite number of times. If a program includes a division calculation that divides by a variable holding the value zero, the system will produce a divide-by-zero error.

```
INTERACTIVE SESSION

>>> 3/0
Traceback (most recent call last):
  File "<pyshell#2>", line 1, in <module>
    3/0
ZeroDivisionError: division by zero
>>>
```

SYLLABUS CHECK

Problem-solving and design: identify errors in given algorithms and suggest ways of removing these errors.

10.04 IDE Debugging Tools and Diagnostics

Many IDEs include sophisticated diagnostics designed to identify possible bugs and provide the user with supportive error messages. These tools are only able to identify errors in the code, not in the logic of the code, and as a result are unable to identify logical errors. IDLE and Wing IDE 101 provide debugging support for both syntax and runtime errors.

Syntax Diagnostics

Syntax errors can be spotted by noticing that the colour of your code in your IDE is not appropriate. For example, if you forget to close the quotation marks at the end of a String, the code will remain green in IDLE until the end of the line. IDLE has a helpful *Check Module* command in the *Run* menu that will find the first instance of an error, highlight it in red and give you an indication of what the problem is, as shown in Figure 10.01.

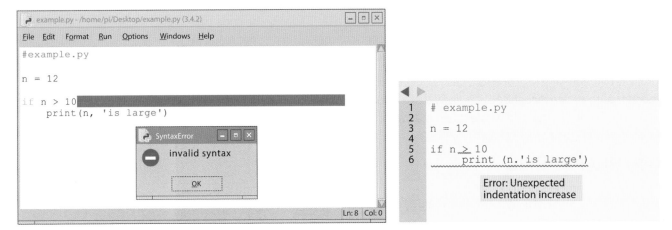

Figure 10.01 Error message in IDLE

Figure 10.02 Error message detail in Wing IDE 101

In this instance, the colon is missing from the end of the line. In Wing IDE 101, this kind of error is shown underlined with a zig-zag line similar to the spell-checker feature in a word processor. Rolling the cursor over the error provides further information, as shown in Figure 10.02.

Runtime Diagnostics

Runtime errors are detected during execution of a program and specific error messages are provided. In Figure 10.03, the `input()` function returns a String variable, but the programmer has tried to use the input in a calculation. The IDE cannot detect that error – it would only occur at runtime (see Figure 10.03).

Figure 10.03 IDLE runtime error showing in Shell window

10.05 Identifying Logical Errors

While the IDE is able to support programmers with syntax and runtime errors, it cannot identify logical errors. The system will operate and process data by following the code that has been written – it is unable to determine if the code contains logical errors that result in unexpected outputs.

The process of identifying logical errors has to be part of the testing process. When unexpected outputs are recognised, it is likely that a logical error will be present in the code. The actual error will also have to be identified manually.

10.06 Dry Running

Dry running is the process of working through a section of code manually to locate logical or runtime errors. This type of testing often uses a trace table to record values within a system during its operation. The values traced could relate to the inputs, outputs or variables used in the process. It is usual to use a table with the variables listed as columns and their changing values recorded in rows.

> **SYLLABUS CHECK**
>
> **Problem-solving and design:** use trace tables to find the value of variables at each step in an algorithm.

Tracing Pseudocode

The following pseudocode algorithm is intended to calculate the quotient division (also known as Integer division) of x by y.

```
w ← 0
INPUT x
INPUT y

WHILE x > y DO
    x ← x – y
    w ← w + 1
ENDWHILE

OUTPUT w
```

DEMO TASK

Trace Table

Complete the trace table (Table 10.01) when the input values are x = 50 and y = 15.

Comments have been added to Table 10.01 to help explain the trace table. Comments are not normally required in a formal trace table.

Table 10.01

x	y	w	Output	Comments
		0		Initialisation value.
50	15	0		The new values are input.
35	15	1		x is reduced by 15, w is incremented by 1. ENDWHILE returns to the WHILE condition check. As x > y, the loop continues to run.
20	15	2		x is reduced by 15, w is incremented by 1. ENDWHILE returns to the WHILE condition check. As x > y, the loop continues to run.
5	15	3		x is reduced by 15, w is incremented by 1. ENDWHILE returns to the WHILE condition check. As x < y, the loop exits.
			3	The value in w is output.

Task 1 – Trace Table Extension

The pseudocode algorithm contains a logical error. Complete a trace table with the input values of x = 60 and y = 15 to identify the error.

Tracing a Flowchart

Flowchart Trace Table

Study the flowchart in Figure 10.04 and then complete a trace table (Table 10.02) where the input value is a = 2.

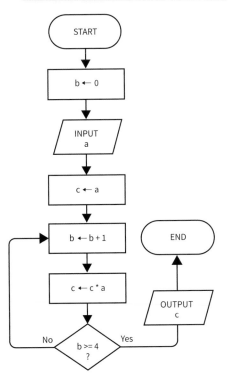

Table 10.02

a	b	c	Output	Comments
	0			Initialisation value
2	0	0		Input a
2	1	2		c ← a b ← b + 1 Will loop as b < 4
2	1	4		c ← c * a Will loop as b < 4
2	2	8		b ← b + 1 c ← c * a Will loop as b < 4
2	3	16		b ← b + 1 c ← c * a Will loop as b < 4
2	4	32		b ← b + 1 c ← c * a Loop exited as b = 4
2	4	32	32	Output value in c

Figure 10.04 Flowchart for a trace table

EXTENSION TASK

Task 2 – Discussion Question

a   What is the aim of this flowchart?

b   What kind of loop is being suggested here?

10.07 Breakpoints, Variable Tracing and Stepping Through Code

Although the IDE cannot identify logical errors, it does provide tools that assist the programmer in the manual process. IDLE and Wing IDE 101, in common with many IDEs, provide the programmer with the ability to execute the program one line at a time, displaying the values held in variables at each step. To allow the programmer to check particular segments of code, the system can be set to execute as normal until it meets a 'breakpoint'. These are created by the programmer, and will cause the system to run a line of code at a time.

In Wing IDE 101 this process is controlled by the buttons shown in Table 10.03.

Table 10.03

Button	Action
🐞	Start or continue debugging until the next breakpoint is reached.
↓	Start debugging at the first line (or step into the current execution point).
→	Execute the current line of code and then wait.
↗	Step out of the current function or method. (Useful if there is a long iteration present.)

The following algorithm has been designed to calculate the number of tins of paint required to cover a wall. The user inputs the length and height of the wall in metres and also the area that can be covered by one tin of paint. The algorithm does not produce the expected result.

```
length = int(input('Enter the length in metres: '))
height = int(input('Enter the height in metres: '))
coverage = int(input('How many square metres are covered by 1 tin? '))

area = length + height
tins = int(area / coverage)
```

The programmer decides to use the breakpoint diagnostic tool to help identify the error. The breakpoint is to be inserted after the input sequence as the programmer is happy that the correct inputs are being obtained. To test the system the programmer decides to use a length of 5 metres, a height of 2 metres and a coverage of 8 square metres per tin of paint; the expected area is 10 square metres.

To insert the breakpoint in Wing IDE 101 all that is required is to click with the cursor, next to the desired line number, in this case line 5. When the bug (🐞) is clicked, the code is executed in the normal fashion until the breakpoint is reached. The values of the various variables are viewable in the _Stack Data_ panel. If a variable contains a value, hovering over the variable name will also show the value it currently contains.

To execute to line 5 and pause, the _step into current execution point_ button (⬇) is clicked. This results in the screen shown in Figure 10.05.

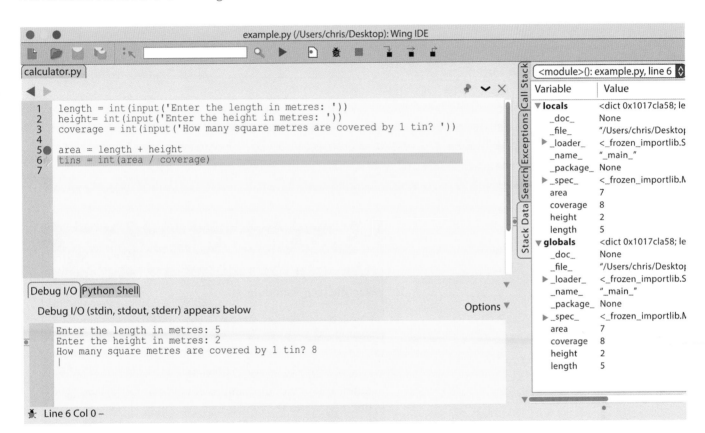

Figure 10.05 Wing IDE showing breakpoint variable values

The breakpoint is indicated by the red circle in line 5 and the next line to be executed is highlighted in pink. To delete a breakpoint click on it again.

In Figure 10.05, it can be seen that the area is 7, not the expected 10. This leads the programmer to identify the error in the calculation of area. They have incorrectly used addition (5 + 2 = 7), not the expected multiplication (5 * 2 = 10).

In IDLE, similar functionality can be achieved by following these steps:

- After writing your script and saving it somewhere, return to the Python Shell. The _Debug_ menu is only available when the Shell window has focus (click on the Shell window to bring it to the front).

- From the _Debug_ menu select _Debugger_.

- Return to the script file window and either _right-click_ or _ctrl-click_ on the line of code beginning with `area =` to create a breakpoint which will be shown by the line being highlighted.

99

- From the *Run* menu, choose *Run Module* or press *F5*, which will start executing the program with the *Debugger* on.

- Click the *Go* button in the *Debugger Control* window. The buttons on the *Debug Control* window function in a similar way to the buttons in Wing IDE 101. To keep track of the values in your variables, it is necessary to at least have the *Locals* and *Globals* checkboxes selected. See Figure 10.06 to see what the process looks like in IDLE running on a Raspberry Pi.

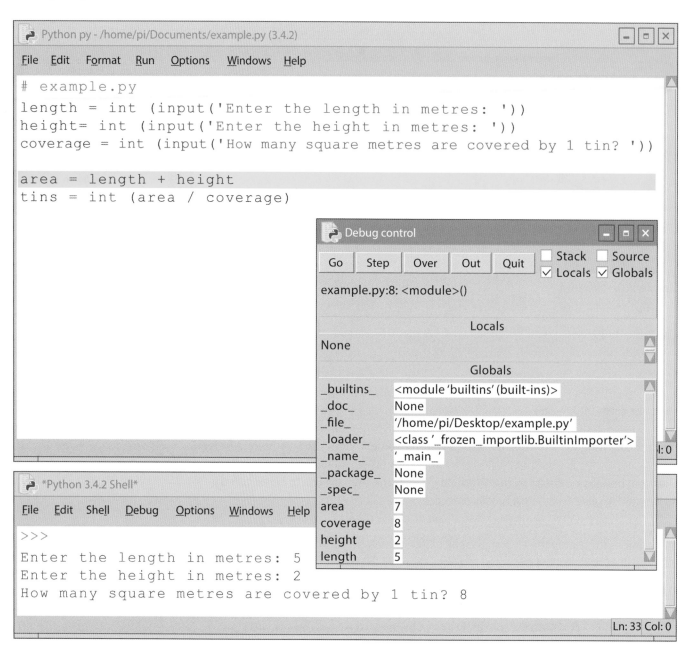

Figure 10.06 IDLE running with the Debugger on

Task 3 – Breakpoint

Once this error was fixed, the programmer continued to receive unexpected outputs for some test values.

a Copy the code into a script in your IDE and, using breakpoints and a range of data, identify the remaining error.

b Decide how you might correct this error.

10.08 Beta Testing

A formal test schedule is designed to test all possible events that a system could experience. It will test normal expected operation as well as extreme inputs or usage. The test schedule will identify the elements of the system to be tested and the data to be used in the tests. Each set of test data and the expected outcome is known as a 'test case'. The data used will fall into three categories, as described in Table 10.04. The example data in Table 10.04 is based on a system designed to determine the grade achieved by students in an examination, with inputs of student marks and the maximum possible mark.

SYLLABUS CHECK

Problem-solving and design: suggest and apply suitable test data.

Table 10.04

Type of test	Description	Example data
Valid data	Data that is expected to be met in the normal operation of the system. It meets the expected validation rules. The system should produce the expected outcome.	Integer values between zero and the maximum possible score.
Invalid data	Data that will not form part of the expected input range. The system should reject the data and output appropriate error messages.	Non-Integer values (it is not possible to get half a mark). Values less than zero or more than the maximum score. Textual inputs, such as 'TEN'.
Boundary data	Data that is at the boundary of the criteria that determine the path of execution of code.	Data that falls at grade boundaries. The grade boundary for an A is 80% and the maximum mark is 100. Data one mark below the grade boundary: 79. Data one mark above the grade boundary: 81.

Task 4 – Beta testing

A system holds the mobile phone number and age next birthday of current patients in a hospital. Mobile telephone numbers are entered as NNNNN-NNNNNN where N is a number. For each of the data items, decide on:

a the appropriate data type

b appropriate validation that could be applied

c invalid and, where appropriate, boundary data that could be used to test input validation.

10.09 Testing Tasks

Task 5

Study the flowchart in Figure 10.07.

Create a trace table showing the values of the variables x, y and w during execution of the algorithm and the output for the following input values:

a   x = 16 and y = 7

b   x = 10 and y = 5

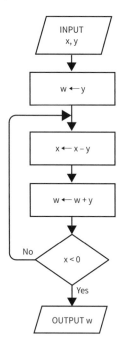

Figure 10.07   Flowchart for task 5

Task 6

The following algorithm is designed to calculate the factorial of a number. It contains a number of logical errors. Identify three errors **and** explain how they could be corrected. You may like to use a trace table to help identify the errors.

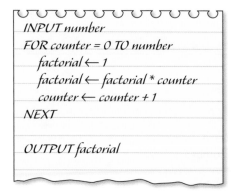

```
INPUT number
FOR counter = 0 TO number
    factorial ← 1
    factorial ← factorial * counter
    counter ← counter + 1
NEXT

OUTPUT factorial
```

Problem-solving and design: identify errors in given algorithms and suggest ways of removing these errors.

Task 7

The following algorithm is designed to accept a series of numbers with the sequence being ended by the user inputting a negative number. At the end of the sequence, the system will output the smallest number input and the sum of the numbers input. The algorithm contains a number of logical errors. Identify the errors **and** explain how they could be corrected.

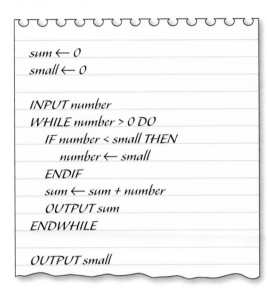

```
sum ← 0
small ← 0

INPUT number
WHILE number > 0 DO
    IF number < small THEN
        number ← small
    ENDIF
    sum ← sum + number
    OUTPUT sum
ENDWHILE

OUTPUT small
```

TIP
There are five different logical errors to identify.

Task 8

A local athletics club holds the following data about individual athletes:

- height (in metres)
- ID (a five-digit membership identification number)
- surname.

For each of the data items, identify:

a the appropriate data type

b an appropriate validation check

c invalid and, where appropriate, boundary data that could be used to test the validation.

Summary

- It is important to test systems to ensure they will perform as expected.

- Alpha testing is completed during the programming of a system.

- Beta testing is formal testing once the system has been completed.

- Logical errors are errors in the logic of the process performed by the code. The code will run but will produce unexpected results. These need to be debugged manually using, for example, trace tables.

- Syntax errors are errors in the syntax used within the code. It is likely that these will be identified by the IDE diagnostics.

- Runtime errors only become apparent during the execution of the code. Attempting to divide by zero is a common runtime error.

- IDEs identify syntax errors and runtime errors. They also provide useful tools to help debug logical errors by providing such facilities as the ability to step through code and add breakpoints.

- Trace tables provide a structure by which the value of variables, inputs and outputs can be traced at each step of an algorithm. They can be helpful in identifying logical errors.

- Valid data is met by the system in its normal operation.

- Invalid data is data that the system is not expecting. The system should identify and reject invalid data and provide appropriate error messages.

- Boundary data is data that falls at the boundaries of value changes. It is used to check the logic of the comparisons used to determine those value changes.

Chapter 11:
Arrays

Learning objectives

By the end of this chapter you will understand how to:

- define an array using flowcharts and pseudocode
- declare and use an array
- read from and write values to an array
- use a number of arrays to organise data
- use Python's list data type as a substitute for arrays when implementing your algorithms.

11.01 What is an Array?

An **array** is a data structure that can hold a set of data items under a single identifier. Just as a variable holds data and is identified by a name, so an array also holds data of a specific type and is referred to by its name or label. While a variable can only hold one data value, an array can hold several values. For example, if you wished to store the surnames of 25 students you could either do this in 25 variables or a single array.

KEY TERMS

Array: A data type that can hold a set of data items of the same sort under a single identifier.

An array is an example of a container data type. Python does not support arrays out of the box. If arrays are required then the array built-in library must be imported first. This is because Python has a rich set of alternative container data types called tuples, lists and dictionaries. You will see later in this chapter that the Python version of the FOR loop is designed to work very closely with these container data types.

It is recommended that, when implementing your pseudocode and flowchart solutions in Python, you use lists to replicate arrays. A list can do everything an array can do and more. For example, lists are able to store a variety of data types at the same time and can be lengthened or shortened as required.

It is worth noting that, although lists are more flexible than arrays, arrays are more efficient for most simple processes.

11.02 Declaring an Array

Declaring an array is a similar process to declaring a variable. The difference is that you need to define the size of the array, determined by the number of data items that the array is required to hold. Each individual value held within an array is identified by an index number. Index numbers are sequential and, in Python, as with many other programming languages, the numbering starts from zero.

Table 11.01 is a diagrammatic representation of an array designed to hold the first five letters of the Greek alphabet.

Table 11.01

Index number	0	1	2	3	4
Data item	Alpha	Beta	Gamma	Delta	Epsilon

The pseudocode format for declaring an array capable of holding the five values is as follows. Note how the range of indices is 0 to 4:

```
greek_letter[0:4] OF String
```

Not all languages number array items from zero and you may see an example of arrays that start from 1. In this example the final index would then become 5:

> greek_letter[1:5] OF String

When writing pseudocode, either method of numbering is acceptable; however, it is vital to remain consistent when using arrays in algorithms. If the array is declared as [0:4] then the following pseudocode must also follow that format with the first data item held in index 0 and the fifth data item in index 4.

SYLLABUS CHECK

Data structures: declare the size of one-dimensional arrays.

The syntax for declaring a list (the array substitute recommended for implementing your algorithms in Python) is:

```
my_list = [None]*4
```

Python's list container does not have to store a declared number of data items. This means that the syntax for creating an empty list of a given length does not look a lot like the pseudocode array declaration. The code above creates an array with four empty data spaces and is equivalent to

> my_array[0,3]

in pseudocode.

If you are not sure how this works, start an interactive session and enter the line of code above. To see what has been created add the following line:

```
print(my_list)
```

FURTHER INFORMATION

Python programmers would normally just declare an empty list such as

```
my_list = []
```

to which data items can be added as required.

11.03 Initialising Arrays

At some point you will want to create an array that is ready filled with content. In pseudocode, it is achieved like this:

> greek_letters ← ['Alpha', 'Beta', 'Gamma', 'Delta', 'Epsilon']

This is now a predefined array with five spaces that will only store Strings. In Python, the equivalent code would be:

```
greek_letters = ['Alpha', 'Beta', 'Gamma', 'Delta', 'Epsilon']
```

11.04 Using Arrays

Arrays offer programmers advantages over simple variables. As we have seen, they allow many data items to be stored under a single identifier. They give the programmer the ability to reference any individual data item by the appropriate **array index** and to use iteration to perform read, write or search operations by looping through the data items. This makes arrays particularly effective when working with data records.

> **KEY TERMS**
>
> **Array index:** A sequential number that references an item in an array.

> **SYLLABUS CHECK**
>
> **Data structures:** show understanding of the use of a variable as an index of an array.

Reading and Writing Data Items

To read a data item, you reference it by the array name and the index number. For example,

```
greek_letters[2]
```

holds the data item 'Gamma'. The same logic applies when writing values to an array. The following code would write the letter 'C' to the specified index position, replacing the original data item:

```
greek_letter[2] = 'C'
```

The syntax in Python for these two operations, using lists, is identical to the pseudocode.

Integer array

Declare an array named 'task' that is capable of holding four Integers. Write code to allow the user to input an Integer to selected array positions. Then add code to allow the user to output the value held in a selected array position.

Figure 11.01(a) shows the flowchart for the input process and Figure 11.01(b) shows the flowchart for the output process. Figure 11.02 shows the corresponding pseudocode for these processes.

START
task[0:3]
INPUT
index
data_item
task[index]
←
data_item
END
(a)
START
INPUT
index
OUTPUT
task[index]
END
(b)

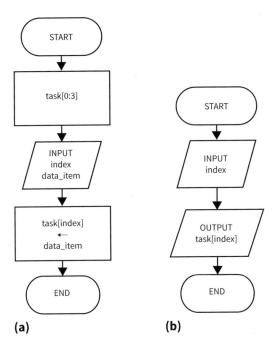

Figure 11.01 Array input (a) and output (b) flowchart

// Input Pseudocode
task[0:3]
INPUT index, data_item
task[index] ← data_item
(a)
// Output Pseudocode
INPUT index
OUTPUT task[index]
(b)

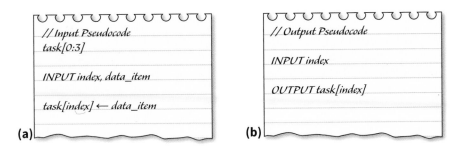

Figure 11.02 Array input and output pseudocode

A Python GUI application can be used to produce the system. The interface could be designed as shown in Figure 11.03. A button runs the subroutines for each of the input and output processes. `Entry` widgets accept the input and display the output. As the functions are so simple, the opportunity has been taken to demonstrate a little more tkinter GUI code.

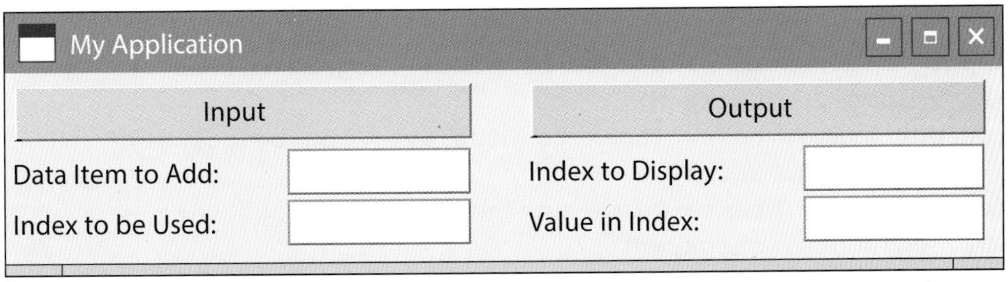

My Application
Input
Output
Data Item to Add:
Index to be Used:
Index to Display:
Value in Index:

Figure 11.03 A GUI interface design

Producing GUI based applications is outside the syllabus.

```
from tkinter import *

# Declare list globally to allow both subroutines access to it
task = [None] * 4

# Functions
def input_data():
    # collect values from Entry boxes
    data_item = int(tbox1.get())
    index = int(tbox2.get())
    # insert new value into array
    task[index] = data_item

def output_data():
    # collect index required
    index = int(tbox3.get())
    # clear output text box and display value
    tbox4.delete(0, END)
    tbox4.insert(END, task[index])

#### Build the GUI
# padding is added to some widgets:
# ipadx adds internal padding to left and right
# padx adds external padding to left and right
window = Tk()
window.title('My Application')
bg_colour = 'linen'

# Create two frames
input_frame = Frame(window, bg=bg_colour)
input_frame.grid(row=0, column=0, ipadx=5, ipady=5)
output_frame = Frame(window, bg=bg_colour)
output_frame.grid(row=0, column=1, ipadx=5, ipady=5)

# Create the labels
input_label1 = Label(input_frame, text='Data Item to Add:', bg=bg_colour)
input_label1.grid(row=1, column=0, sticky=W)
input_label2 = Label(input_frame, text='Index to be Used:', bg=bg_colour)
input_label2.grid(row=2, column=0, sticky=W)
output_label1 = Label(output_frame, text='Index to Display:', bg=bg_colour)
output_label1.grid(row=1, column=0, sticky=W)
output_label2 = Label(output_frame, text='Value in Index:', bg=bg_colour)
output_label2.grid(row=2, column=0, sticky=W)

# Create the buttons
inputButton = Button(input_frame, text='Input', command=input_data, width=24)
inputButton.grid(row=0, column=0, columnspan=2, padx=5, pady=5)
outputButton = Button(output_frame, text='Output', command=output_data, width=24)
outputButton.grid(row=0, column=0, columnspan=2, padx=5, pady=5)
```

```
# Create the textboxes
tbox1 = Entry(input_frame, width=10)
tbox1.grid(row=1, column=1)
tbox2 = Entry(input_frame, width=10)
tbox2.grid(row=2, column=1)
tbox3 = Entry(output_frame, width=10)
tbox3.grid(row=1, column=1)
tbox4 = Entry(output_frame, width=10)
tbox4.grid(row=2, column=1)

# start tkinter loop
window.mainloop
```

Reading from and Writing to an Array

Build the Integer array application and then try to write or read data with index 4. Try to input a textual value into the array. Both these actions will cause the system to crash and output an error message.

Task 1

What are the appropriate validation methods that could be used to prevent the user entering these types of invalid data?

Task 2

Draw a flowchart and create a pseudocode algorithm that includes these validation techniques.

Task 3

Test that your algorithm works by programming and running the code in Python and using suitable test data.

TIP

At some point, you may wish to know exactly what is in your array. In Python, all container data types can be printed to the console with a simple print statement. Sometimes it can be useful to insert such a print statement in your application's code when testing to print out the current state of your array. Look at this interactive session to see how it works:

```
>>> letters = ['a', 'b', 'c']
>>> print(letters)
['a', 'b', 'c']
>>>
```

Iteration in Arrays

The process of reading individual array positions can be extended by using a loop to read all the positions in an array. This allows iterative code to be used to check multiple data values.

Where the size of the array is known, a FOR loop can achieve the required iterative process. The counter variable in the FOR loop can be used to iterate through the index positions.

Data structures: read or write values in an array using a FOR . . . TO . . . NEXT loop.

The following pseudocode shows how iteration can be used to output all the data items in a ten-item array:

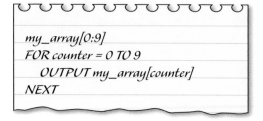

```
my_array[0:9]
FOR counter = 0 TO 9
    OUTPUT my_array[counter]
NEXT
```

DEMO TASK

Letters

Declare an array called 'letters' that is capable of holding six single characters. Initialise the array with letters a to f. Write code that allows the user to search the array to identify if any letter input by the user is in the array or not.

Figure 11.04 shows a flowchart and pseudocode for the algorithm.

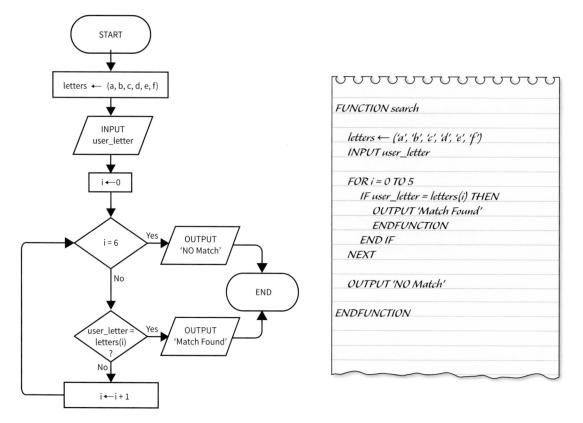

```
FUNCTION search

    letters ← ('a', 'b', 'c', 'd', 'e', 'f')
    INPUT user_letter

    FOR i = 0 TO 5
        IF user_letter = letters(i) THEN
            OUTPUT 'Match Found'
            ENDFUNCTION
        END IF
    NEXT

    OUTPUT 'NO Match'

ENDFUNCTION
```

Figure 11.04 Flowchart and pseudocode for search algorithm

The FOR loop condition has been set to follow the declaration of the array, which has an index from 0 to 5. Once a match has been found the subroutine is ended. The 'No match' message is only shown if the loop has completed.

The following coded solution is a text-based implementation of the letters algorithm in Python. To illustrate how this works, a call to the function has been added after the function definition:

```python
def search():
    # Initialise list to be searched
    letters = ['a','b','c','d','e','f']

    user_letter = input('Enter the character to search for: ')

    # Perform search of letters
    for i in range(0,6):
        if user_letter == letters[i]:
            print('Match found.')
            return

    print('No match.')

# Call function
search()
```

FURTHER INFORMATION (Optional)

The Python Way

There are many different programming languages. They all have their advantages and disadvantages. One of Python's strengths is the way it works with container variables. You may recall that the reason we use the **range()** function in the FOR loop is because Python FOR loops are of the iterative kind rather than the more traditional counter FOR loop. Python's FOR loop iterates through sequences or containers – **range()** creates a sequence of numbers. **letters** is already a container and so can be handled directly by Python's FOR loop. This kind of FOR loop is designed to loop through all items in the container irrespective of its length because lists, unlike arrays, can change length. The normal Python way of looping through letters would be like this:

```python
# Perform search of letters
for letter in letters:
    if user_letter == letter:
        print('Match found.')
        return
```

Indeed Python is so adept at handling containers there is no need to use a FOR loop at all. Instead Python programmers would simply use the **in** keyword:

```python
# Perform search of letters
if user_letter in letters:
    print('Match found.')
else:
    print('No match.')
```

Furthermore, as a String in Python is also a container data type, where all characters and spaces are indexed from zero, the following would also appear to function in the same way:

```
# Initialise string to be searched:
letters = 'abcdef'

search = input('Enter the character to search for: ')

# Perform search of letters
if search in letters:
    print('Match found.')
else:
    print('No match.')
```

Note that this is searching through a String data type and not an array. It is nice to know that all the methods you are learning about arrays are also useful in Python when manipulating String variables.

It would be a disservice to the reader, in a book on Python, not to point out its strengths. As a computer science student, however, you are required to iterate through arrays using a counter in a FOR loop. So when implementing your array algorithms, use the format in the solution shown above this further information box.

TASKS

Using iteration with an Array

The current system will stop once a match is found. This would be an ideal situation if the values are all unique, but this may not be the case.

For tasks 4 and 5, initialise the letters array with the following data items:

letters ← ('a', 'a', 'b', 'c', 'c', 'c')

Task 4

Draw a flowchart and create a pseudocode algorithm for a 'search' function that searches the entire array to check for multiple matches. The output should be the number of occasions a match was found.

Task 5

Test that your algorithm works by programming and running the code in Python.

11.05 Groups of Arrays

If you need to hold multiple data elements for each data record, it is possible to use arrays in groups. Provided that the same index number is used in each array for equivalent data items, multiple data items can be read. Consider a situation where a system holds the records shown in Table 11.02.

Table 11.02

Student ID	Surname	Computing grade
1001	Morgan	A
1002	Smith	C
1003	Jones	B

These data items could be held in three arrays as shown in Tables 11.03, 11.04 and 11.05 with the same index position in each array referring to the data regarding one record. As ID 1002 is held at index position 1 in the ID array, the remaining data for that record is held in index position 1 in the other two arrays.

Table 11.03 Student ID array

Index	0	1	2
Data item	1001	1002	1003

Table 11.04 Surname array

Index	0	1	2
Data item	Morgan	Smith	Jones

Table 11.05 Computing grade array

Index	0	1	2
Data item	A	C	B

The pseudocode to output the Surname and Grade for a given Student ID would be as follows:

```
INPUT search_ID
FOR i = 0 TO 2
    IF search_ID = ID[i] THEN
        OUTPUT surname[i]
        OUTPUT grade[i]
    ENDIF
NEXT
```

Multidimensional Arrays and Other Containers

Programmers are not limited to one-dimensional arrays. It is possible to have arrays that can hold more than one set of data. It is worth pointing out that with Python's rich set of container data types, there are more elegant ways of solving the problem outlined at the beginning of this section. Indeed, the flexibility of Python's container data types and the libraries of methods that work with them is comprehensive. Lists, for example, can expand and contract; they can contain a mixture of data types including other containers. Dictionaries provide a kind of unordered list where the programmer chooses the key (instead of being limited to indexes of 0,1,2, etc.). These keys could be a String or number type variable and can contain a mixture of data types, including other containers. And of course, as discussed earlier, Strings can be treated as container data types in Python. By learning Python, you have a very powerful programming language at your disposal.

Both multidimensional arrays and Python's other containers are beyond the scope of the syllabus and this book. If you are interested in learning more about Python's container data types you might like to try one of the Coding Club level two books which explore Python's containers in a less formal way. (Find out more at http://codingclub.co.uk.)

11.06 Array Reference for Implementation in Python

Items can then be added using simple index calls:

Declaring an empty '"array' of length 4:	
Pseudocode:	Python code:
my_array[0:3] OF <data type>	``` my_list = [None]*4 print(my_list) output: [None, None, None, None] ```

Items can be assigned using simple index calls:

Pseudocode:	Python code:
my_array[0] ← 2 *my_array[1] ← 4* *my_array[2] ← 6* *my_array[3] ← 8*	``` my_list[0] = 2 my_list[1] = 4 my_list[2] = 6 my_list[3] = 8 ```

Items can be accessed using simple index calls:

Pseudocode:	Python code:
OUTPUT my_array[0] Output: *2*	``` print(my_list[0]) Output: 2 print(my_list) Output: [2, 4, 6, 8] ```

Iterate through an array with a For Loop:

Pseudocode:	Python code:

FOR counter = 0 TO 3 THEN
    OUTPUT my_array[counter]
NEXT
Output:
2
4
6
8
	``
	for counter in range(0,4):
	        print(my_list[counter])
	``
	Output:
	2
	4
	6
	7

11.07 Array Tasks

Task 6

a Draw a flowchart and create a pseudocode algorithm that iterates through an array of Integers and outputs the average. Declare and initialise the array with the following set of Integers: 12, 14, 10, 6, 7, 11 and 3.

b Test that your algorithm works by programming and running the code in Python.

Task 7

An algorithm will take an Integer value, n. It will call a subroutine to place into an array 12 incremental multiples of n (the first array index will hold $1 \times n$ and the last index position $12 \times n$). An additional subroutine will allow the user to output all the multiples in order.

a Draw a flowchart and create pseudocode for this algorithm.

b Test that your algorithm works by programming and running the code in Python.

Task 8

The data in Table 11.06 is to be organised in arrays so that the user can search via User ID and the system will display all the data related to that User ID.

Table 11.06

User ID	Age	Gender
112	45	Male
217	16	Female
126	27	Female

a Draw a flowchart and create a pseudocode algorithm that accepts a User ID and displays the related data.

b Test that your algorithm works by programming and running the code in Python.

Summary

- An array is a variable that can hold a set of data items, of the same data type, under a single identifier.

- When an array is declared, its size is defined. In Python indexes start from zero.

- Each element or data item in an array can be referenced by its index.

- The index can be used to read or write values in an array.

- A FOR loop can be used to iterate through the index locations in an array. The loop counter is used to identify successive index numbers.

- Holding records which consist of more than one data item can be achieved by the use of multiple arrays. Data for each record is held at the same index position in the different arrays.

- When using Python to implement algorithms involving arrays, a list is used as a substitute for an array.

Chapter 12:
Pre-release Task Preparation

Learning objectives

By the end of this chapter you will understand how to:

- work through your pre-release tasks for Paper 2
- combine top-down design and standard methods of solution to produce efficient algorithms
- combine all you have learnt about testing and validation to produce effective algorithms
- produce efficient and effective flowcharts, pseudocode and Python scripts

Paper 2 in the IGCSE starts with an extended question about the tasks presented in the pre-release material that is made available to students a few months in advance of sitting the actual paper. Although no pre-prepared material is allowed to be taken into the exam, it is very important that the pre-release material is carefully studied and worked through. These pre-release tasks are duplicated in the exam paper.

This chapter will take you through an example of such a task which has been written by the author.

12.01 The tasks

The first job is to carefully read the tasks and think through how they might be approached.

DEMO TASKS

Example pre-release assignment

You should attempt all of the following **programmming** tasks.

A coach needs to keep a record of the total number of shots, assists and goals her squad of 30 players achieved in the season. She wants to be able to use this to compare the progress of the players and the club from season to season, and to select the player of the year.

Write and test a program for the coach. Your program should include:

- Meaningful names for variables, constants and other identifiers.
- Prompts for data entry.
- Clear output and error messages.

You will need to complete the following three tasks:

TASK 1 – Set up arrays

Set-up one-dimensional arrays to store:

- Player names
- Player scores for Shots, Assists and Goals
  - Maximum shots possible in a season is 100
  - Maximum assists possible in a season is 50
  - Maximum goals in a season is 40
- A success index for each student

Input and store the names for 30 players.

Input and store the players' scores for Shots, Assists and Goals. Validate all the scores on entry, any invalid scores should be rejected.

TASK 2 – calculate the success index

Calculate the season success index for each student and store it in the array using this formula:

$$\text{Success Index} = (1 \times \text{assists}) + (2 \times \text{shots}) + (3 \times \text{goals})$$

Calculate the average success index for the whole squad.

Output each players' name followed by their squad index. Output the average squad index for the squad.

TASK 3 – Select the player of the season

Select the player with the highest squad index and output their name, goals scored, assists, shots and success index.

12.02 Apply top-down design

Having read through the tasks we now apply our decomposition skills using a top-down design approach. When this is completed we will have produced a structured diagram that will help us formulate our final solution.

Before looking at the structured diagram provided below, try and do this yourself. It may help to look back at Chapter 8. (In this case study, we are following the process outlined in section 8.05 in Chapter 8.)

When you have produced your own structured diagram, have a look and compare with Figure 12.01. Note that there is no right answer at this stage.

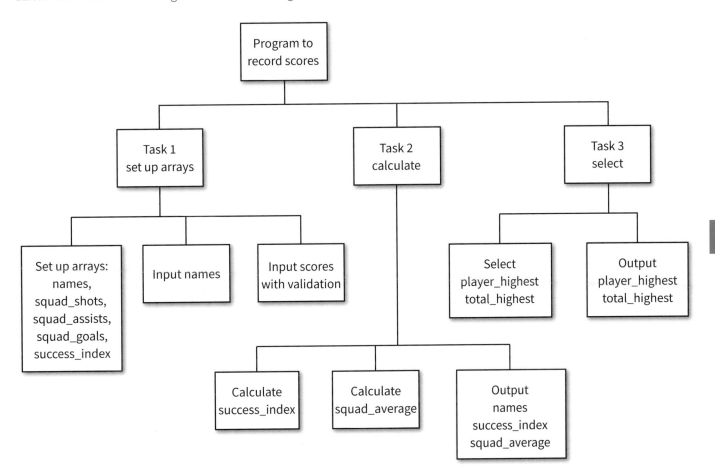

Figure 12.01 Initial structure diagram

12.03 Set up the arrays

The first step in TASK 1 is to set up the arrays. It simplifies the algorithm if this is done outside of the flowchart but will, of course, need to be in the Python scripts. Please note that not all pre-release tasks will require the use of arrays.

Can you remember how to do this using the preferred IGCSE structure? Have a go before looking at the solution shown below in Figure 12.02. If you need a reminder, section 11.06 in Chapter 11 might help.

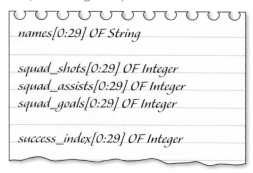

```
names[0:29] OF String

squad_shots[0:29] OF Integer
squad_assists[0:29] OF Integer
squad_goals[0:29] OF Integer

success_index[0:29] OF Integer
```

Figure 12.02 Pseudocode showing the five arrays required for TASK 1

12.04 Flowchart and pseudocode for TASK 1

Producing the flowchart and pseudocode algorithms for TASK 1 should not be beyond you at this stage. Again have a go at this before referring to the provided answer. If you are a bit rusty with respect to handling arrays, Chapter 11 should help. Don't forget to validate the numerical input (see Chapter 9 for a reminder of how to do this). The answer can be seen in Figure 12.03.

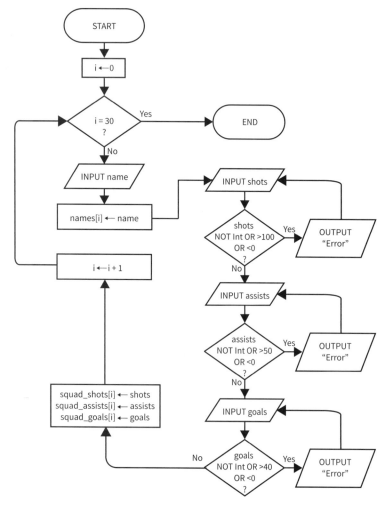

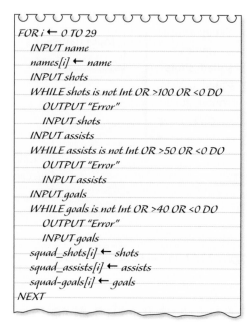

```
FOR i ← 0 TO 29
    INPUT name
    names[i] ← name
    INPUT shots
    WHILE shots is not Int OR >100 OR <0 DO
        OUTPUT "Error"
        INPUT shots
    INPUT assists
    WHILE assists is not Int OR >50 OR <0 DO
        OUTPUT "Error"
        INPUT assists
    INPUT goals
    WHILE goals is not Int OR >40 OR <0 DO
        OUTPUT "Error"
        INPUT goals
    squad_shots[i] ← shots
    squad_assists[i] ← assists
    squad-goals[i] ← goals
NEXT
```

Figure 12.03 A flowchart and pseudocode for TASK 1

Task 1

Write a working Python implementation of the algorithm shown in Figure 12.03 or that of your own algorithm for TASK 1. At the end of your script, add extra code to print out the contents of the three arrays. Test that it works by changing the number of iterations from 30 to 3.

Note: To present a realistic scenario the answer provided in Chapter 14 works but will not pass a strict testing regime. This is picked up and corrected in sections 12.07 and 12.08.

12.05 Adding TASK 2 efficiently

It can be tempting to consider the pre-release tasks separately and indeed the initial decomposition process encourages this. Therefore, for TASK 2, we might start by thinking about iterating through the players' names and then using the corresponding array index to find their three scores as a separate process. We would then use these to produce each players' success index and load these into the `success _ index[]` array, which would all be achieved in a new loop. However, after a little thought, it will become obvious that we have already iterated through all the required data in the solution to TASK 1. Therefore, the requirements for TASK 2 can be accomplished in the same FOR LOOP you produced earlier.

To obtain the squad average, we could iterate through the `success _ index[]` array, calculating as we go along but again we can do this in the same loop. Thus, an efficient way of completing TASK 2 is to add the required processes to the flowchart from TASK 1.

Again it is recommended that you try and do this yourself before looking at the answer provided in Figure 12.04. To make the new algorithm clearer, the validation from TASK 1 has been removed.

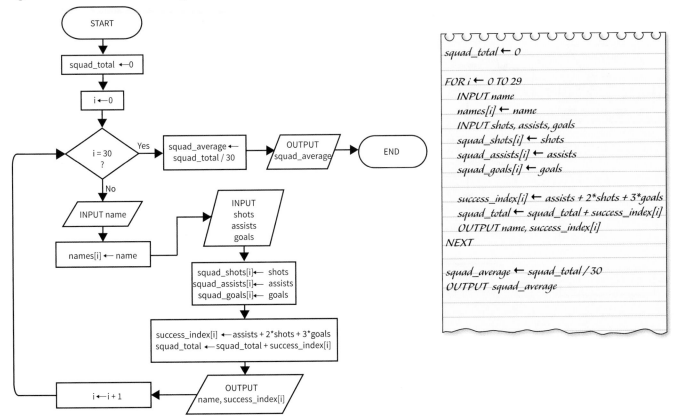

Figure 12.04 A flowchart and pseudocode for TASKS 1 and 2 (without validation)

Task 2

Write a working Python implementation of the algorithm shown in Figure 12.04 or that of your own algorithm for TASKS 1 and 2.

12.06 Adding TASK 3 to the system

By now it is clear that TASK 3 might also be accomplished within the same iteration. To achieve this it is necessary to initialise two more global variables to store the highest success index and the name of the player that achieved it. An IF clause can be used to test each success index in turn and update the global variables if required. Again try and adjust your flowchart and pseudocode without looking at the solution provided in Figure 12.05.

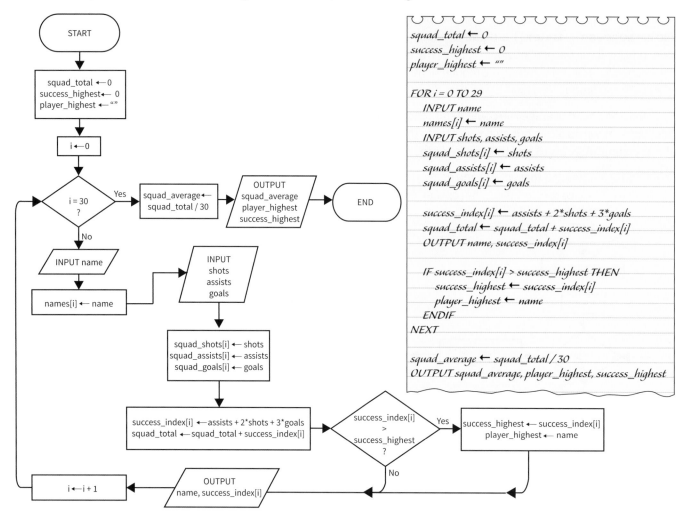

Figure 12.05 A flowchart and pseudocode for TASKS 1,2 and 3 (without validation)

Task 3

Write a working Python implementation of the algorithm shown in Figure 12.05 or that of your own algorithm for TASKS 1, 2 and 3.

12.07 Coding and testing

By now you will have realised that most of the work involved in building a coded solution takes place during the planning and computational thinking. Once an algorithm is produced, the coding is relatively simple to write. However the job is not complete until the implementation has gone through some systematic testing. It is now time to think about what possible test data you could try out on your Python script. Then the final program will need to fix any problems encountered.

Task 4 – Test data

Create a set of test data that you can use to check that your implementation works as expected. The data set should include: normal data, erroneous data and extreme and boundary data.

TIP

When testing your Python Code it is a good idea to reduce the number of students in your class so that not too much test data has to be tried. In this case, changing the number of loops to three times and then calculating your average by dividing by 3 makes testing a lot easier. Don't forget to put your figures back to what is required after you have finished testing.

12.08 A final implementation

Producing the final Python implementation will have been relatively simple, except for coding the validation. Repeatedly testing that the numerical input is an integer, rather than text, makes the code quite long. As such, you probably found, like I did, that it was best to pull the validation code out into a function. This also has the benefit of making code readability and maintenance easier in the future.

It turned out to be a lot simpler to validate the raw input before casting to an integer (as had been done in TASK 1). Did you find a more efficient way of doing this?

Here is one possible implementation in Python:

```python
# prereleaseEG.py
# This script provides one solution to the IGCSE example pre-release task

# Initialise the empty "arrays":
names = [None]*30
squad_shots = [None]*30
squad_assists = [None]*30
squad_goals = [None]*30
success_index = [None]*30

# Initialise global variables
squad_total = 0
success_highest = 0
player_highest = ""
```

```
# Validation function
def validate_score(score, score_type):
    # test for integer
    try:
        int(score)
    except:
        return False

    # range test
    if score_type==1 and (int(score) > 100 or int(score) < 0):
        return False
    if score_type==2 and (int(score) > 50 or int(score) < 0):
        return False
    if score_type==3 and (int(score) > 40 or int(score) < 0):
        return False

    # pass tests
    return True

#### Main Loop
for i in range(30):
    # get inputs and validate all numerical data
    name = input("Enter player's name: ")
    names[i] = name

    shots = input("Enter shots made: ")
    while validate_score(shots, 1) is False:
        print("Error: Unexpected input")
        shots = input("Enter shots made: ")

    assists = input("Enter assists made: ")
    while validate_score(assists, 2) is False:
        print("Error: Unexpected input")
        assists = input("Enter assists made: ")

    goals = input("Enter goals scored: ")
    while validate_score(goals, 3) is False:
        print("Error: Unexpected input")
        goals = input("Enter goals scored: ")

    # load the "arrays"
    squad_shots[i] = int(shots)
    squad_assists[i] = int(assists)
    squad_goals[i] = int(goals)

    # process scores
    success_index[i] = squad_assists[i] + 2*squad_shots[i] + 3*squad_goals[i]
    squad_total = squad_total + success_index[i]
```

```
    # print current player's success_index
    print(name, success_index[i])

    # keep track of highest scoring player
    if success_index[i] > success_highest:
        success_highest = success_index[i]
        player_highest = name

# Calculate squad average
squad_average = squad_total / 30

# Print final summary
print("\nSquad average:", squad_average)
print("Most successful player:", player_highest, "with", success_highest)
```

12.09 Alternative solutions

It is important to note that the exam board sets tasks that do not have just one solution. This is also the case with the example presented at the beginning of this chapter. In the rest of the chapter a narrative has been provided for the development of one of only many possible solutions. You should be clear that there is more than one possible solution and, if your solution differs to that of the author's, this does not mean that it is wrong. For example, it may be more convenient for the coach to enter all of the goals for all of the players first and then add the assists and shots later. The solution provided here does not cater for this. Alternatively she may want to add the scores for 10 players, save these entries and then enter the other players' scores later. Again another solution would be required. On a simpler level, the choice of whether to enter the goals before assists and shots is completely arbitrary as is the order of validation.

Summary

- It is important to thoroughly work through the pre-release tasks for Paper 2 thoroughly.

- These tasks will require you to combine top-down design and standard methods of solution to produce efficient algorithms.

- It is necessary to apply all you have learnt about testing and validation to produce effective algorithms.

- It is necessary to produce efficient and effective flowcharts, pseudocode and Python implementations of the tasks in your pre-release material.

Chapter 13 Examination Practice

This is a series of examination-style questions. At the end of Chapter 14 there is a mark scheme which provides examples of correct solutions. It also indicates how the marks might be awarded for programming questions; there is often more than one correct solution. The exam-style questions and accompanying answers have been written specifically for this book.

13.01 Questions

Question 1

Consider the following algorithm:

```
INPUT Size
INPUT Country

IF Country = 'UK' THEN
      Size ← Size + 2
      OUTPUT Size
ELSE
      IF Country = 'USA' THEN
            Size ← Size / 2
      ELSE
            OUTPUT Size
      ENDIF
ENDIF
```

What size will be output for the following inputs?

Size	Country	Output
20	USA	
19	France	
14	UK	

[3]

Question 2

This section of pseudocode loops through an array called Num which already holds 50 positive numbers. The index of the first number is index 1. The code will output the smallest number.

```
Small ← 0
FOR Counter = 1 TO 50
      IF Num(Counter) < Small THEN
            Num(Counter) ← Small
      ENDIF
      Counter ← Counter + 1
      OUTPUT Small
NEXT
```

There are four errors in this code.

Locate these errors and suggest a corrective piece of code.

[8]

Question 3

The following pseudocode inputs the time taken to complete a 100-metre sprint.
A value of –1 stops the input. The information output is the average time taken and the number of runs that took 20 or more seconds.

```
Count ← 0
Number ← 0
Total ← 0

INPUT Time

WHILE Time > 0
    Total ← Total + Time
    IF Time >= 20 THEN
        Number ← Number + 1
    ENDIF
    Count ← Count + 1
    INPUT Time
ENDWHILE

Average ← Total / Count
OUTPUT Average, Number
```

Complete the trace table for the following sequence of input values:

18, 19, 24, 21, 18, 17, 23, 20, 19, 21, -1.

Time	Total	Number	Count	Average	Output
18	18		1		
19	37		2		
24	61	1	3		
21	82	2	4		
18	100		5		
17	117		6		
23	140	3	7		
20	160	4	8		
19	179		9		
21	200	5	10		
-1				20	20, 5

[6]

Question 4

Write an algorithm using pseudocode or draw a flowchart, which inputs three Integers, N1, N2 and N3, and outputs the smallest of the three numbers.

[3]

Question 5

One type of validation is a presence check. Suggest other validation techniques that could be used for the following data inputs. For each technique give an example of invalid data that could be used to test the validation rule.

Data input	Validation technique	Invalid test data
Mobile phone number		
Height of a person		
Number of brothers		

[6]

Question 6

The flowchart inputs a sequence of numbers: a value below zero stops the input.

Complete the trace table for the input data: 11, 9, −2

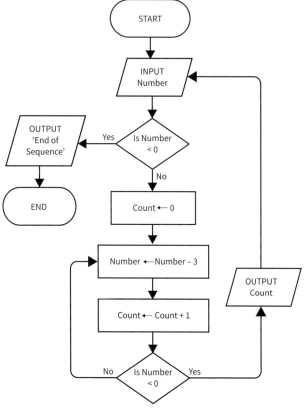

Figure 13.01 Flowchart for Question 6

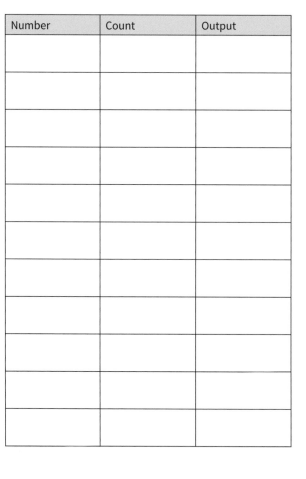

Number	Count	Output

[4]

Question 7

A floor turtle uses these instructions:

Instruction	Meaning
FORWARD *d*	Move *d* cm forward
BACKWARD *d*	Move *d* cm backward
LEFT *t*	Turn left *t* degrees
RIGHT *t*	Turn right *t* degrees

Instruction	Meaning
REPEAT *n*	Repeat the next set of Instructions *n* times
ENDREPEAT	End of the REPEAT loop
PENUP	Raise the pen (stop drawing)
PENDOWN	Lower the pen (start drawing)

Figure 13.02 Target shape for Question 7

Each square in the drawing is 10 cm by 10 cm.

Complete the set of instructions to draw the shape (shown in bold lines).

    PENDOWN
    RIGHT 90
    REPEAT 3
    . . .

[4]

Question 8

The flowchart shows the system used at a set of automatic crossing gates on a junction of a railway and a road. The system constantly checks for a signal sent from an approaching train. When the signal is received the system activates warning lights and, after a period of time, closes the gates unless traffic is on the crossing. When the crossing gates are closed the train is sent an approach signal. The system will open the gates once the train has passed unless another train is approaching.

Complete the flowchart using the following instructions. **Only use** the instruction numbers to complete the flowchart.

Instruction number	Instruction
1	Has Train Passed?
2	Wait 15 Seconds
3	Warning Lights OFF
4	Warning Lights ON
5	Gates CLOSE
6	Crossing Clear?
7	Signal Received?

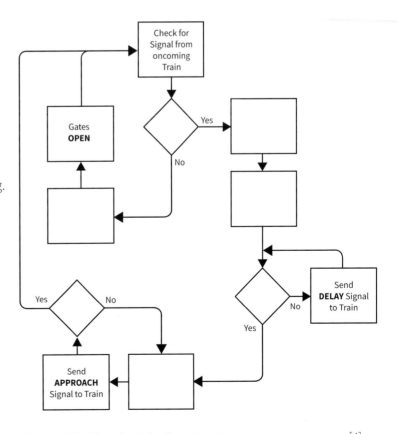

Figure 13.03 Flowchart for Question 8

[4]

Question 9

The following data about a group of students is to be stored in three arrays:

Name[1:6]
ID[1:6]
Score[1:6]

Name	ID	Score
David	D167	120
Alan	A447	96
Manjit	M892	112
Jatinder	J098	100
Barrac	B492	99
Taona	T873	103

Write an algorithm using pseudocode which:

- inputs a target score

- outputs the Name and ID of all students who have a score higher than the target score. [3]

Question 10

Abdulla requires a system to check if a four-digit number meets the following rules:

- The sum of the digits must not be a multiple of 5.

- The sum of the first two digits must not be less than the sum of the last two digits.

For example:

- 6423 is invalid because 6 + 4 + 2 + 3 = 15 which is a multiple of 5.

- 3256 is invalid because 3 + 2 is less than 5 + 6.

Write an algorithm using pseudocode or draw a flowchart which takes four single digits as input and outputs 'VALID' or 'INVALID' to indicate if the input meets the above rules. [5]

Chapter 14 Solutions

Chapter 2 – Sequence

Task 1

The flowchart is shown in Figure 14.01.

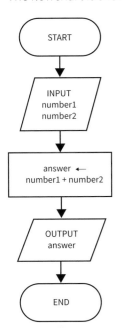

Figure 14.01 Flowchart for Task 1

Chapter 3 – Variables and Arithmetic Operators

Task 1

Either use a **print()** function:

```
>>> print(c)
0.42857142857142855
```

or in interactive mode you can simply type **c**:

```
>>> c
0.42857142857142855
```

Task 2 – Addition Machine

There is only one character that needs changing in the code to turn the Multiplication Machine into an Addition Machine:

```
# Request and store user input
number1 = int(input('Please insert first number: '))
number2 = int(input('Please insert second number: '))

result = number1 + number2
```

```
# Display the value held in the variable result
print('The answer is', result)

# End nicely by waiting for the user to press the return key.
input('/n/nPress RETURN to finish.')
```

All numerical values will remain Integers.

Task 3 – Volume of Water in Aquarium

The algorithm is shown in Figure 14.02.

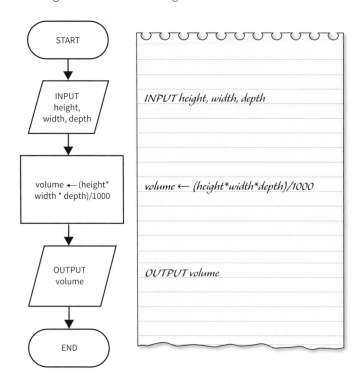

Figure 14.02 Flowchart and pseudocode for Task 3

Here is a possible Python implementation:

```
# Request and store user input
height = int(input('Enter the height of the aquarium in centimetres: '))
width = int(input('Enter the width of the aquarium in centimetres: '))
depth = int(input('Enter the width of the aquarium in centimetres: '))

# Calculate volume in litres
volume = (height * width * depth)/1000

# Display the value held in the variable volume
print('The volume in litres = ', volume)

# End nicely
input('\n\nPress RETURN to finish.')
```

Task 4 – Area and Circumference of a Circle

The algorithm is shown in Figure 14.03.

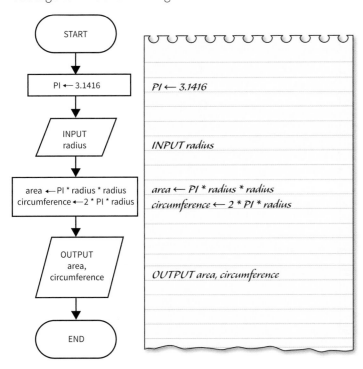

Figure 14.03 Flowchart and pseudocode for Task 4

Here is a possible Python implementation:

```python
# Declare PI as a constant
PI = 3.1416

# Request and store user input
radius = int(input('Enter the radius: '))

# Calculate the outputs
area = PI * radius * radius
circumference = 2 * PI * radius

# Display the values held in area and circumference
print('The area of the circle is ', area)
print('The circumference of the circle is ', circumference)

# End nicely
input('\n\nPress RETURN to finish.')
```

Task 5

The algorithm is shown in Figure 14.04.

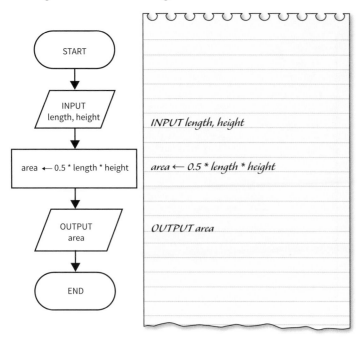

Figure 14.04 Flowchart and pseudocode for Task 5

Here is a possible Python implementation:

```python
# Request and store user input
length = int(input('Enter the length of the base: '))
height = int(input('Enter the height: '))

# Calculate area
area = 0.5 * length * height

# Display the value held in the variable area
print('The area of the triangle is ', area)

# End nicely
input('\n\nPress RETURN to finish.')
```

Task 6

The algorithm is shown in Figure 14.05.

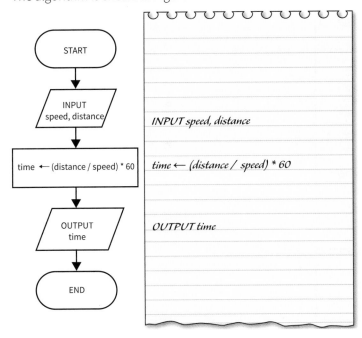

Figure 14.05 Flowchart and pseudocode for Task 6

Here is a possible Python implementation:

```python
# Request and store user input
speed = int(input('Enter the average speed: '))
distance = int(input('Enter the distance: '))

# Calculate time in minutes
time = (distance / speed)*60

# Display the value held in the variable time
print('The journey duration is', time, 'minutes.')

# End nicely
input('\n\nPress RETURN to finish.')
```

Task 7

The algorithm is shown in Figure 14.06.

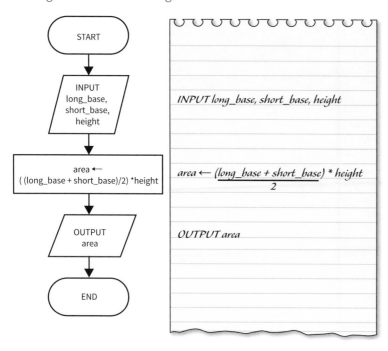

Figure 14.06 Flowchart and pseudocode for Task 7

Here is a possible Python implementation:

```python
# Request and store user input
long_base = int(input('Enter the length of the longest base: '))
short_base = int(input('Enter the length of the shortest base: '))
height = int(input('Enter the height of the trapezium: '))

# Calculate the area
area = ((long_base + short_base) / 2)* height

# Display the value held in the variable area
print('The area of the trapezium is', area)

# End nicely
input('\n\nPress RETURN to finish.')
```

Task 8

The algorithm is shown in Figure 14.07.

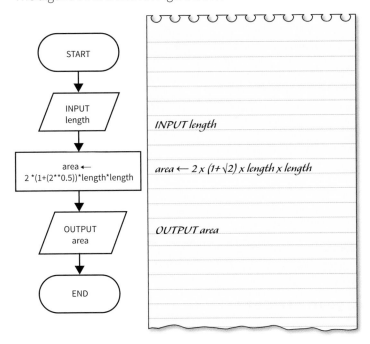

Figure 14.07 Flowchart and pseudocode for Task 8

Here is a possible Python implementation:

```python
# Request and store user input
length = int(input('Enter the length of the side: '))

# Calculate the area
area = 2*(1+(2**0.5))*(length**2)

# Display the value held in the variable area
print('The area of the octagon is', area)

# End nicely
input('\n\nPress RETURN to finish.')
```

Chapter 4 – Subroutines

Task 1

The following pseudocode models the algorithm:

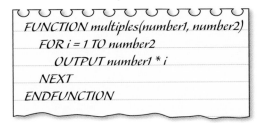

Task 2

The following pseudocode models the algorithm:

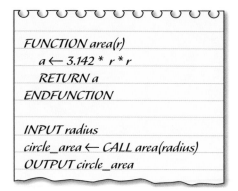

```
FUNCTION area(r)
    a ← 3.142 * r * r
    RETURN a
ENDFUNCTION

INPUT radius
circle_area ← CALL area(radius)
OUTPUT circle_area
```

Here is a possible Python implementation:

```python
def area(r):
    a = 3.142 * r * r
    return a


radius = int(input('What is the radius of your circle? '))


circle_area = area(radius)
print('The area of your circle is', circle_area)
```

Task 3

The algorithm for the function is shown in Figure 14.08.

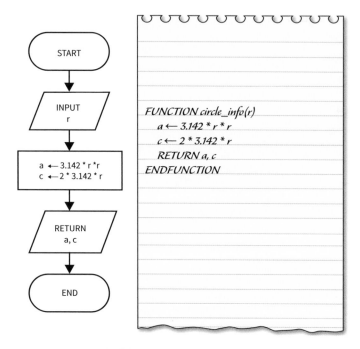

```
FUNCTION circle_info(r)
    a ← 3.142 * r * r
    c ← 2 * 3.142 * r
    RETURN a, c
ENDFUNCTION
```

Figure 14.08 Flowchart and pseudocode for Task 3

Here is a possible Python implementation:

```python
def circle_info(r):
    a = 3.142 * r * r
    c = 2 * 3.142 * r
    return a,c

radius = int(input('What is the radius of your circle? '))

area, circumf = circle_info(radius)

print('The area of your circle is', area)
print('The circumference of your circle is', circumf)
```

Task 4

The algorithm for the function is shown in Figure 14.09.

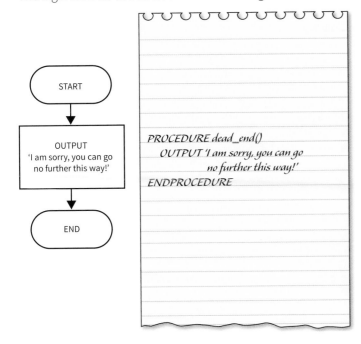

```
START

OUTPUT
'I am sorry, you can go
no further this way!'

END
```

```
PROCEDURE dead_end()
    OUTPUT 'I am sorry, you can go
            no further this way!'
ENDPROCEDURE
```

Figure 14.09 Flowchart and pseudocode for Task 4

Here is a possible Python implementation:

```python
def dead_end():
    print('I am sorry, you can go no further this way!')

dead_end()
```

Chapter 5 – GUI Applications (Optional)

Task 1 – Tkinter Widgets

Selected example GUI applications with a variety of widgets are shown below.

A text entry box is shown in Figure 14.10.

Figure 14.10 A GUI with a text entry box and a label

```
from tkinter import *

window = Tk()
window.title('My Application')

Label(window, text='Name:').grid(row=0, column=0)
my_text_box = Entry(window, width=20)
my_text_box.grid(row=0, column=1)

window.mainloop()
```

Frames are shown in Figure 14.11.

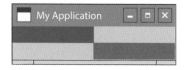

Figure 14.11 A GUI with two frames

```
from tkinter import *

window = Tk()
window.title('My Application')

frame1 = Frame(window,height=20, width=100, bg='green')
frame1.grid(row=0, column=0)
frame2 = Frame(window,height=20, width=100, bg='red')
frame2.grid(row=1, column=1)

window.mainloop()
```

Producing GUI based applications is outside the syllabus.

142

A drop-down menu is shown in Figure 14.12.

Figure 14.12 A GUI with a drop-down menu

```
from tkinter import *

window = Tk()
window.title('My Application')
window.geometry('200x50')

options = (1,2,3)
my_variable_object = IntVar() # access the value with .get()
my_variable_object.set('choose:')
my_dropdown = OptionMenu(window, my_variable_object, *options)
my_dropdown.grid()

window.mainloop()
```

Task 2 – Drop-down Menu

The drop-down menu is shown in Figure 14.13.

Figure 14.13 A GUI application with a drop-down menu

```
from tkinter import *

def change_text():
    my_label.config(text=gender.get())

# Create the main tkinter window
window = Tk()
window.title('My Application')

# Add an empty tkinter label widget and place it in a grid layout
my_label = Label(window, width=25, height=1, text='')
my_label.grid(row=0, column=0)

# Add a tkinter button widget
my_button = Button(window, text='Submit', width=10, command=change_text)
my_button.grid(row=1, column=0)
```

```
# Create a tkinter string variable object to store the selected choice
gender = StringVar()

# Add a drop-down widget
options = ('female', 'male')
gender.set('choose:')
my_dropdown = OptionMenu(window, gender, *options)
my_dropdown.grid()

# Enter the main loop event
window.mainloop()
```

Chapter 6 – Selection

Task 1

The output would be the same. The crucial values to consider are where `number1` and `number2` are equal. In the original example, when the numbers are equal, `number2` is not greater than `number1` so the system will report 'First'. We would of course prefer it to output 'Same'.

Task 2

a The logic will need to change to `IF number2 >= number 1`.

b If the criteria was reversed to `IF number1 <= number 2`, the same output would be achieved.

Task 3

a An `if...elif...else` construct is not as efficient as a CASE statement because all of the conditions above the one that returns True have to be checked. The rest are then skipped. This makes it as efficient as the Nested IF solution. CASE statements are more efficient than this as they jump straight to the condition that returns True because they actually do not test any of them; the separate cases are in fact indexed locations in memory.

b CASE statements are limited to evaluating the output from a single variable.
An `if...elif...else` construct is more flexible because it can have different test conditions at each new `elif` clause.

Task 4 – Simple Calculator

A Python implementation for this task is shown here:

```
from tkinter import *

# Initialise global variable
operator = ''

# functions
def set_A():
    global operator
    operator = 'A'
```

```python
def set_S():
    global operator
    operator = 'S'

def set_M():
    global operator
    operator = 'M'

def set_D():
    global operator
    operator = 'D'

def evaluate():
    number1 = float(textbox1.get())
    number2 = float(textbox2.get())
    textbox_ans.delete(0.0, END)   # clear output text box
    if operator == 'A':
        textbox_ans.insert(END, number1+number2)
    elif operator == 'S':
        textbox_ans.insert(END, number1-number2)
    elif operator == 'M':
        textbox_ans.insert(END, number1*number2)
    elif operator == 'D':
        textbox_ans.insert(END, number1/number2)
    else:
        textbox_ans.insert(END, 'Incorrect operator.')

# Build the GUI
window = Tk()
window.title('Calculator')

# Create the labels
label1 = Label(window, text='Number1:').grid(row=0, column=0, columnspan=2,
sticky=W)
label2 = Label(window, text='Number2:').grid(row=0, column=2, sticky=W)
label3 = Label(window, text='Answer:').grid(row=3, column=2, sticky=W)

# Create two text entry boxes
textbox1 = Entry(window, width=10)
textbox1.grid(row=1, column=0, columnspan=2, padx=(0,5), sticky=W)
textbox2 = Entry(window, width=10)
textbox2.grid(row=1, column=2, sticky=W)

# Create a text output box
textbox_ans = Text(window, width=14, height=1, bg='light green')
textbox_ans.grid(row=4, column=2, sticky=W)

# Create the operator buttons
button_add = Button(window, text='+', width=3, command=set_A)
button_add.grid(row=2, column=0)
```

```
button_subtract = Button(window, text='-', width=3, command=set_S)
button_subtract.grid(row=2, column=1)
button_multiply = Button(window, text='*', width=3, command=set_M)
button_multiply.grid(row=3, column=0)
button_divide = Button(window, text='/', width=3, command=set_D)
button_divide.grid(row=3, column=1)
button_equals = Button(window, text='=', width=6, command=evaluate)
button_equals.grid(row=4, column=0, columnspan=2)

window.mainloop()
```

Task 5 – Examination Grading System

The algorithm solution is shown in Figure 14.14.

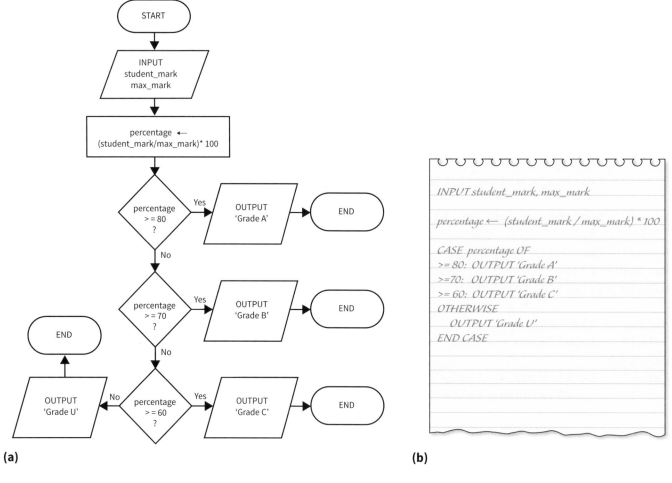

(a)

(b)

Figure 14.14 Flowchart and pseudocode for Task 5

Here is a possible Python implementation:

```
student_mark = int(input('Input STUDENT mark: '))
max_mark = int(input('Input MAXIMUM mark: '))

percentage = (student_mark / max_mark) * 100

if student_mark >= 80:
```

```
    print ('Grade A')
elif student_mark >= 70:
    print ('Grade B')
elif student_mark >=60:
    print ('Grade C')
else:
    print ('Grade U')
```

Task 6 – Parcel Delivery System

The algorithm solution is shown in Figure 14.15.

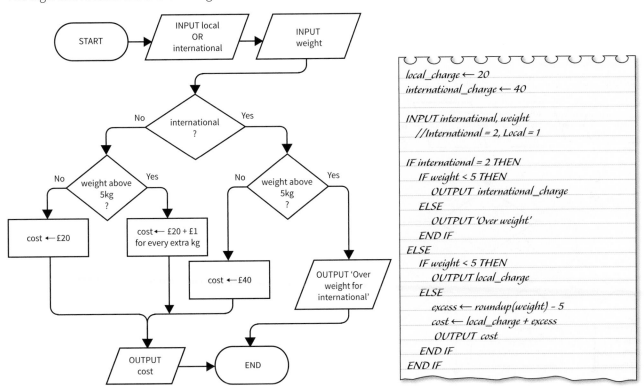

Figure 14.15 Flowchart and pseudocode for Task 6

Here is a possible Python implementation.

```
local_charge = 20
international_charge = 40

international = input('Input "2" for international and "1" for local:')
weight = float(input('Input weight of parcel:'))

# Helper function:
def roundup(n):
    if n - int(n) > 0:
        n = int(n) + 1
    return n

# Algorithm solution
```

```
if international == '2':
    if weight < 5:
        print(international_charge)
    else:
        print('Over weight')
else:
    if weight < 5:
        print(local_charge)
    else:
        excess = roundup(weight) - 5
        cost = local_charge + excess
        print(cost)
```

Task 7 – CO$_2$ Calculator

The algorithm solution is shown in Figure 14.16.

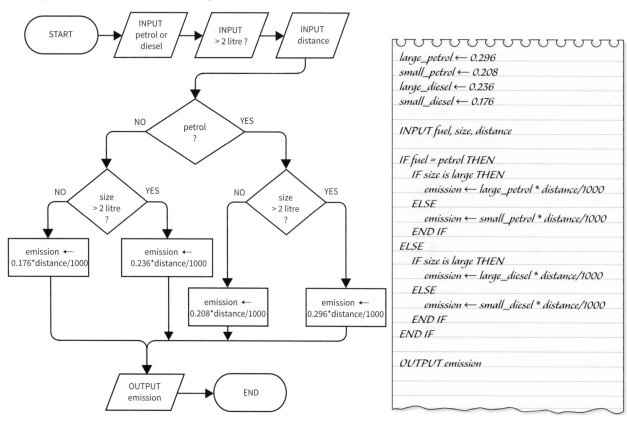

14.16 Flowchart and pseudocode for Task 7

Here is a possible Python implementation:

```
large_petrol = 0.296
small_petrol = 0.208
large_diesel = 0.236
small_diesel = 0.176

fuel = input('Input "P" for petrol and "D" for diesel: ')
size = input('Input "L" for larger than 2 litres and "S" for less: ')
distance = int(input('Input annual mileage: '))
```

148

```
if fuel == 'P':
    if size == 'L':
        emission = large_petrol * distance / 1000
    else:
        emission = small_petrol * distance / 1000
else:
    if size == 'L':
        emission = large_diesel * distance / 1000
    else:
        emission = small_diesel * distance / 1000

print(emission)
```

Task 8 – Improved Calculator

The flowchart algorithm solution is shown in Figure 14.17. The main flowchart is on the left and the Clear button one is on the right.

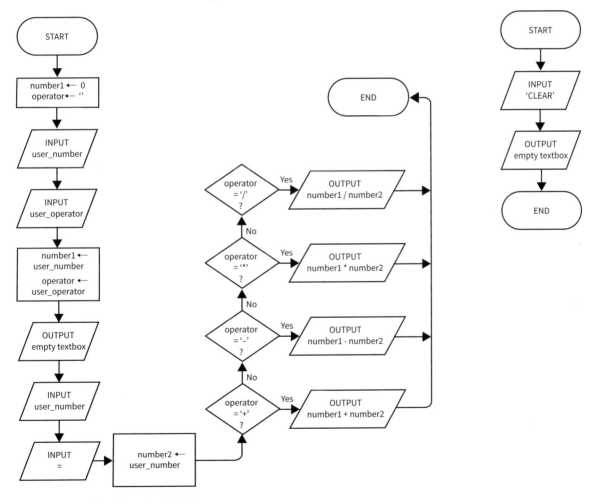

Figure 14.17 Flowchart for Task 8

The following code shows a complete possible Python implementation:

```python
from tkinter import *

# Initialise global variables
operator = ''
number1 = 0

# helper function
def operation(op):
    global number1
    global operator
    number1 = float(textbox.get())
    operator = op
    textbox.delete(0, END)

# button functions
def add():
    operation('+')

def minus():
    operation('-')

def times():
    operation('*')

def divide():
    operation('/')

def clear():
    textbox.delete(0, END)

def evaluate():
    number2 = float(textbox.get())

    # Clear output text box
    textbox.delete(0, END)

    # Complete calculation and display answer
    if operator == '+':
        textbox.insert(END, number1 + number2)
    elif operator == '-':
        textbox.insert(END, number1 - number2)
    elif operator == '*':
        textbox.insert(END, number1 * number2)
    elif operator == '/':
        textbox.insert(END, number1 / number2)
    else:
        textbox.insert(END, 'Error')
```

```
# Build the GUI
window = Tk()
window.title('Calculator')

# Create one text entry box
textbox = Entry(window, width=20)
textbox.grid(row=0, column=0, columnspan=3)

# Create the operator buttons
button_add = Button(window, text='+', width=3, command=add)
button_add.grid(row=2, column=0)
button_subtract = Button(window, text='-', width=3, command=minus)
button_subtract.grid(row=2, column=1)
button_multiply = Button(window, text='*', width=3, command=times)
button_multiply.grid(row=3, column=0)
button_divide = Button(window, text='/', width=3, command=divide)
button_divide.grid(row=3, column=1)
button_equals = Button(window, text='=', width=6, command=evaluate)
button_equals.grid(row=4, column=0, columnspan=2)
button_clear = Button(window, text='CLEAR', width=6, command=clear)
button_clear.grid(row=4, column=2, sticky=E)

# Start tkinter mainloop()
window.mainloop()
```

Task 9 – CO$_2$ Calculator Extension

```
large_petrol = 0.296
small_petrol = 0.208
large_diesel = 0.236
small_diesel = 0.176

fuel = input('Input "P" for petrol and "D" for diesel:')
size = input('Input "L" for larger than 2 litres and "S" for less:')
distance = int(input('Input annual mileage:'))

if fuel == 'P' and size == 'L':
    emission = large_petrol * distance / 1000
elif fuel == 'P' and size == 'S':
    emission = small_petrol * distance / 1000
elif fuel == 'D' and size == 'L':
    emission = large_diesel * distance / 1000
elif fuel == 'D' and size == 'S':
    emission = small_diesel * distance / 1000
else:
    emission = 'Error!'

print(emission)
```

Task 10 – Cumulative Calculator

a This is a complex task with several possible solutions. It could be that you produced separate flowcharts and pseudocode for each function called by each button. Alternatively you may have, as in the Python implementation below, produced a helper function that is called by much simpler button functions. You will, however, have found it very difficult to produce a single flowchart solution as it just gets too big. In these circumstances it is better to produce separate flowcharts for each smaller problem. You will know if your flowchart or pseudocode algorithm was correct if it led to a successfully working Python implementation.

b An example Python implementation for this task is shown below. Note that the GUI parts of the code are omitted as these remain unchanged from Task 8.

```python
# As this calculator does not have a keyboard
# the answers have to be deleted before adding the next number.

from tkinter import *

# Initialise global variables
operator = ''
number1 = 0

# helper function
def operation(op):
    global number1
    global number2
    global operator

    if operator == '':
        number1 = float(textbox.get())
    else:
        number2 = float(textbox.get())
        if operator == '+':
            answer = number1 + number2
        elif operator == '-':
            answer = number1 - number2
        elif operator == '*':
            answer = number1 * number2
        elif operator == '/':
            answer = number1 / number2

        # Update textbox
        textbox.delete(0, END)
        textbox.insert(END, answer)

        # Copy the value of answer to number1 to
        # maintain cumulative total
        number1 = float(answer)
```

```
    # Store latest operator selection
    operator = op

# button functions
def add():
    operation('+')

def minus():
    operation('-')

def times():
    operation('*')

def divide():
    operation('/')

def clear():
    global operator
    global number1
    global number2

    textbox.delete(0, END)
    operator = ''
    number1 = 0.0
    number2 = 0.0

def evaluate():
    global operator
    global number1
    global number2

    number2 = float(textbox.get())

    # Clear output text box
    textbox.delete(0, END)

    # Complete calculation and display answer
    if operator == '+':
        answer = number1 + number2
    elif operator == '-':
        answer = number1 - number2
    elif operator == '*':
        answer = number1 * number2
    elif operator == '/':
        answer = number1 / number2
    else:
        textbox.insert(END, 'Error')

    # Update textbox with answer and reset operator
    textbox.insert(END, answer)
    operator = ''
```

Chapter 7 – Iteration

Task 1

Figures 14.18 and 14.19 show the output screens for a text-based solution and a GUI implementation, respectively.

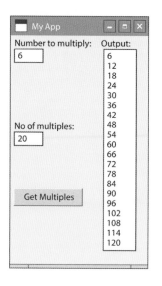

Figure 14.18 Text-based output

Figure 14.19 GUI interface

Producing GUI based applications is outside the syllabus.

The code for the text-based solution:

```python
number = int(input('Input number to multiply: '))
number_required = int(input('Input required number of multiples: '))

for counter in range(1,number_required+1):
    multiple = number * counter
    print(multiple)
```

The code for the GUI application:

```python
from tkinter import *

def multiply():
    # get contents of textbox_input
    number = int(textbox_input1.get())
    number2 = int(textbox_input2.get())

    # clear output text box
    textbox_output.delete(0.0, END)

    # process and output result
    for counter in range(1,number2+1):
        multiple = str(number * counter) + '\n'
        textbox_output.insert(END, multiple)

# Build the GUI
window = Tk()
window.title('My App')
```

154

```
# give the window a size and background colour
window.geometry('200x325')
window.configure(background='linen')

# Create the labels
input_label = Label(window, text='Number to multiply: ', bg='linen')
input_label.grid(row=0, column=0, sticky=W)
input_label2 = Label(window, text='No. of multiples: ', bg='linen')
input_label2.grid(row=2, column=0, sticky=W)
output_label = Label(window, text='Output: ', bg='linen')
output_label.grid(row=0, column=1, sticky=E)

# Create text entry boxes for entering numbers
textbox_input1 = Entry(window, width=5)
textbox_input1.grid(row=1, column=0, sticky=NW)
textbox_input2 = Entry(window, width=5)
textbox_input2.grid(row=3, column=0, sticky=NW)

# Create text box for outputting multiples
textbox_output = Text(window, height=20, width=6)
textbox_output.grid(row=1, column=1, rowspan=5, sticky=E)

# Create the button
multiply_button = Button(window, text='Get Multiples', command=multiply)
multiply_button.grid(row=4, column=0, sticky=W)

window.mainloop()
```

Task 2
The Python code for a text-based implementation is shown here:

```
answer = 1

a = int(input('Enter a: '))
b = int(input('Enter b: '))

for counter in range(b):
    answer = answer * a

print(answer)
```

This could also be implemented more simply without using iteration:

```
a = int(input('Enter a: '))
b = int(input('Enter b: '))

print(a**b)
```

Task 3 – Discussion Question
Limiting the iterations to **number-1** will result in iterations where the counter value is greater than half of the input number. In those situations, it would be impossible to produce a modulus of zero. Limiting the iterations to the rounded Integer value of number / 2 would be more efficient.

Task 4 (Optional)

Figures 14.20 shows the interface of a possible GUI implementation.

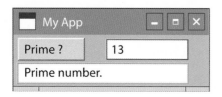

Figure 14.20 GUI interface for primes

The Python code for a possible implementation:

```python
from tkinter import *

def prime():
    modulus_counter = 0

    # Get contents of textbox_input
    number = int(textbox_input.get())

    # Clear output text box
    textbox_output.delete(0.0, END)

    # Run algorithm
    for counter in range(2,number):
        modulus = number % counter
        if modulus == 0:
            modulus_counter = modulus_counter +1

    if modulus_counter == 0:
        textbox_output.insert(END, 'Prime number.')
    else:
        textbox_output.insert(END, 'Not a prime number.')

# Build the GUI
window = Tk()
window.title('My App')

# Give the window a size and background colour
window.geometry('200x50')
window.configure(background='lightgreen')

# Create text entry box for entering number
textbox_input = Entry(window, width=10)
textbox_input.grid(row=0, column=1, sticky=E)

# Create text box for output
textbox_output = Text(window, height=1, width=25)
textbox_output.grid(row=1, column=0, columnspan=2)
```

Producing GUI based applications is outside the syllabus.

```
# Create the button
prime_button = Button(window, text='Prime ?', command=prime)
prime_button.grid(row=0, column=0, sticky=W)

window.mainloop()
```

Task 5

If the line that increases the counter by one is commented out, the program enters an infinite loop. This is because the test used to evaluate the WHILE statement never returns True because **counter** remains equal to 1.

Task 6 – WHILE Loop

Figures 14.21 shows a flowchart and pseudocode solution.

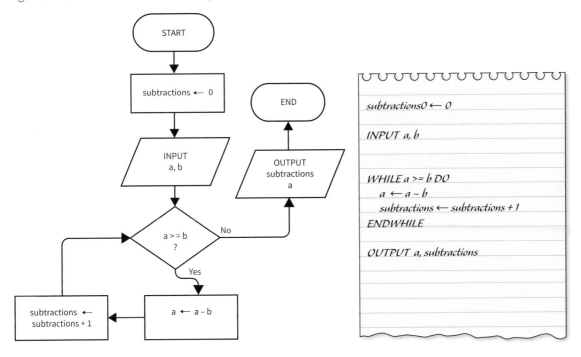

Figure 14.21 Flowchart and pseudocode for Task 6

The Python code for a possible text-based implementation:

```
# Initialise a counter to keep track of the number of subtractions
subtractions = 0

# Get user input as integers
a = int(input('Enter a: '))
b = int(input('Enter b: '))

while a >= b:
    a = a - b
    subtractions = subtractions +1

print('a Quotient b =', subtractions)
print('a Modulus b =', a)
```

Task 7

Here is a text-based Python implementation:

```python
prime = True

number = int(input('Enter your number: '))

counter = 2

while True:
    modulus = number % counter
    if modulus == 0:
        prime = False
    counter = counter+1

    # Loop until check
    if counter == number-1 or prime == False:
        break

if prime == True:
    print('Your number is a prime number.')
else:
    print('Your number is NOT a prime number.')
```

Task 8

Python implementations of the WHILE and REPEAT . . . UNTIL approaches:

```python
total = 0
number = int(input('Enter number: '))

while number != -1:
    total = total + number
    number = int(input('Enter number: '))

print(total)
```

(a)

```python
total = 0
while True:
    number = int(input('Enter number: '))
    total = total + number

    # UNTIL clause
    if number == -1:
        break

total = total +1

print(total)
```

(b)

Chapter 8 – Designing Algorithms

Task 1 – Discussion Question

Other solutions include:

- The IF statement could determine the highest number input before the calculation of total. Both must remain within the loop but the order of completion is not important.

- The FOR loop could have been written as FOR counter = 0 TO 99; this would still iterate 100 times.

- It would have been possible to use a WHILE or REPEAT . . . UNTIL loop. Although a FOR loop is an efficient solution to a scenario where the number of iterations is known, any loop can be written to perform a similar role. Remember that in a FOR loop, the NEXT statement automatically increments the loop counter; WHILE and REPEAT . . . UNTIL loops do not automatically increment the loop counter so this would need to be included in the code.

Task 2

A rather detailed structure diagram for the process is shown below.

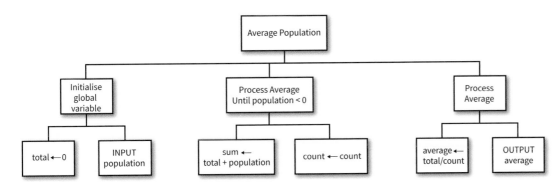

Figure 14.22 Structure diagram

The resultant flowchart and pseudocode are shown in Figure 14.23.

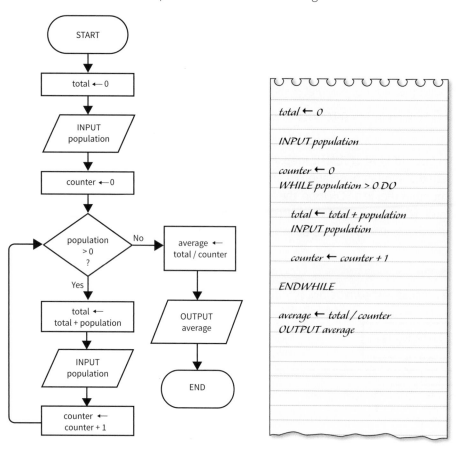

Figure 14.23 Flowchart and pseudocode for Population algorithm

Task 3

Figure 14.24 shows a flowchart and pseudocode algorithm.

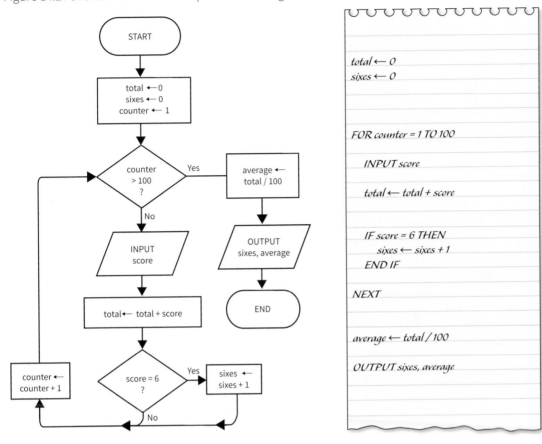

Figure 14.24 Flowchart and pseudocode for Task 3

The following is a text-based Python implementation. To test your code, reduce the iterations to a much smaller number.

```python
total = 0
sixes = 0

for i in range(100):
    score = int(input('Enter the dice score: '))
    total = total + score

    if score == 6:
        sixes = sixes + 1

average = total / 100

print('Sixes:', sixes)
print('Average:', average)
```

Task 4

Figure 14.25 shows a flowchart algorithm.

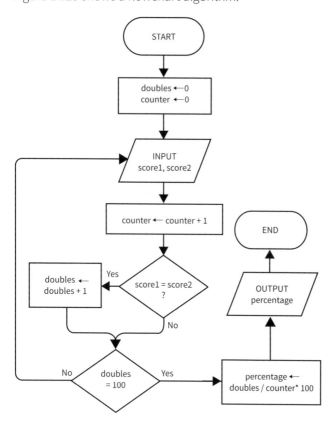

Figure 14.25 Flowchart solution for Task 4

Figure 14.26 shows two pseudocode solutions that could be used to achieve the aim of the algorithm.

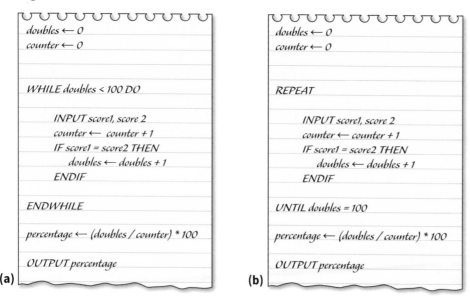

Figure 14.26 Two pseudocode solutions for Task 4

The following is an example of a text-based WHILE loop implementation:

```
doubles = 0
counter = 0

while doubles < 100:
    score1 = int(input('Enter the first dice score: '))
    score2 = int(input('Enter the second dice score: '))

    # To help the user a line return is provided
    print('')

    counter = counter + 1

    if score1 == score2:
        doubles = doubles + 1

percent = (doubles / counter) * 100

print('Percentage doubles thrown:', percent)
```

Task 5

Figure 14.27 shows a flowchart algorithm.

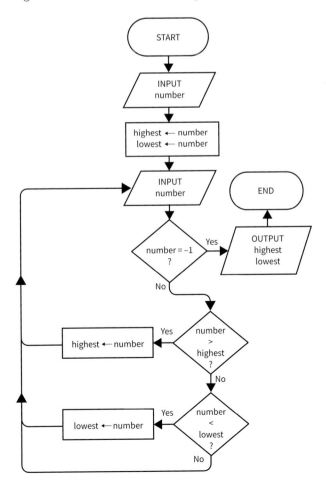

Figure 14.27 Flowchart solution for Task 5

Figure 14.28 shows a two pseudocode solutions that could be used to achieve the aim of the algorithm.

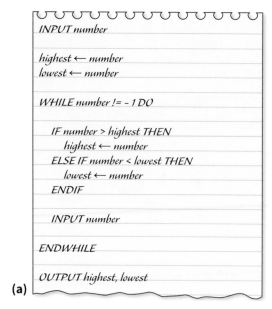

(a)
```
INPUT number

highest ← number
lowest ← number

WHILE number != -1 DO

    IF number > highest THEN
        highest ← number
    ELSE IF number < lowest THEN
        lowest ← number
    ENDIF

    INPUT number

ENDWHILE

OUTPUT highest, lowest
```

(b)
```
INPUT number

highest ← number
lowest ← number

REPEAT

    IF number > highest THEN
        highest ← number
    ELSE IF number < lowest THEN
        lowest ← number
    ENDIF

    INPUT number

UNTIL number = -1

OUTPUT highest, lowest
```

Figure 14.28 Pseudocode solutions for Task 5

The following is an example of a text-based WHILE loop implementation:

```python
number = int(input('Enter a number: '))

highest = number
lowest = number

while number != -1:
    if number > highest:
        highest = number
    elif number < lowest:
        lowest = number

    number = int(input('Enter another number: '))

print('The highest was:', highest)
print('The lowest was:', lowest)
```

The following is an example of a text-based REPEAT ... UNTIL Python implementation:

```python
number = int(input('Enter a number: '))

highest = number
lowest = number

while True:
    if number > highest:
        highest = number
    elif number < lowest:
        lowest = number
```

```
number = int(input('Enter another number: '))

if number == -1:
    break

print('The highest was:', highest)
print('The lowest was:', lowest)
```

Task 6

Figure 14.29 shows a flowchart and pseudocode algorithm.

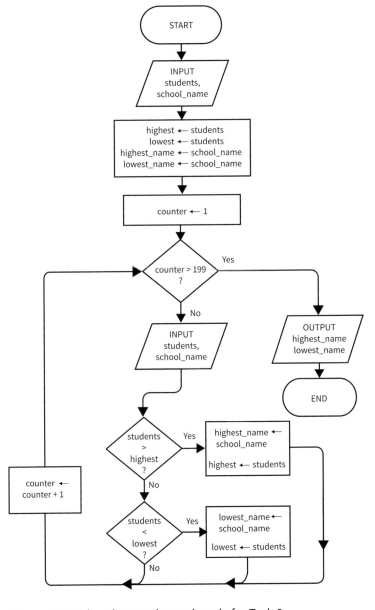
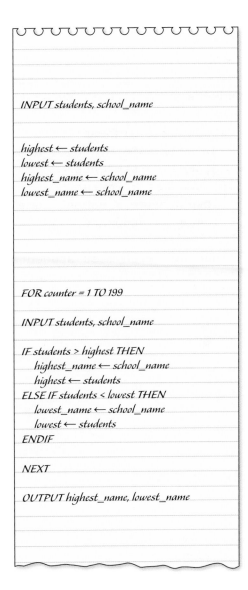

Figure 14.29 Flowchart and pseudocode for Task 6

The index is for 199 iterations rather than 200 because one school has been entered before the loop starts. The following is an example of a text-based Python implementation. You can test your code by setting the number of iterations to 5.

```python
school_name = input('Enter the school name: ')
students = int(input('Enter the number of students: '))

highest = students
lowest = students
highest_name = school_name
lowest_name = school_name

for i in range(199):
    # Add a line return between schools
    print('')

    school_name = input('Enter the school name: ')
    students = int(input('Enter the number of students: '))

    if students > highest:
        highest_name = school_name
        highest = students
    elif students < lowest:
        lowest_name = school_name
        lowest = students

print('\nSchool with most students:', highest_name)
print('School with least students:', lowest_name)
```

Task 7

Figure 14.30 shows a flowchart and pseudocode algorithm using a REPEAT . . . UNTIL loop.

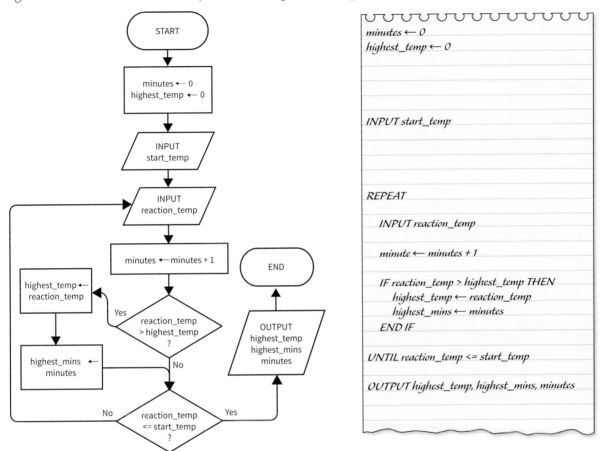

Figure 14.30 Flowchart and pseudocode for Task 7

The following is an example of a text-based Python implementation:

```python
minutes = 0
highest_temp = 0

start_temp = int(input('Enter the start temperature and press ENTER '))

while True:
    # In the scenario this would be automatically input from a sensor
    reaction_temp = int(input())

    minutes = minutes + 1

    if reaction_temp > highest_temp:
        highest_temp = reaction_temp
        highest_mins = minutes

    # UNTIL condition
    if reaction_temp <= start_temp:
        break

print('\nHighest temp:', highest_temp, 'reached at', highest_mins, 'mins')
print('Total reaction time:', minutes)
```

Chapter 9 – Checking Inputs

Task 1

a Figure 14.31 shows a flowchart and pseudocode for the algorithm.

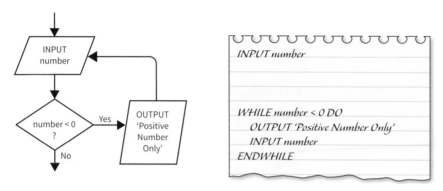

Figure 14.31 Flowchart and pseudocode for Task 1

b The following is an example of a text-based Python implementation:

```python
number = int(input('Insert POSITIVE number: '))

while number < 0:
    number = int(input('Positive numbers only: '))
```

Note that this code does not validate for non-numeric entry. This would have to be validated first.

Task 2

a Figure 14.32 shows a flowchart and pseudocode for the algorithm.

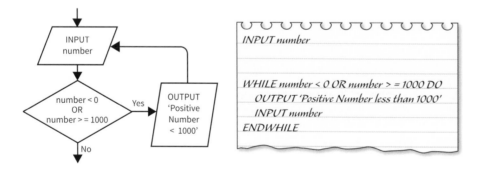

Figure 14.32 Flowchart and pseudocode for Task 2

b The following is an example of a text-based Python implementation:

```python
number = int(input('Insert POSITIVE number: '))

while number < 0 or number >= 1000:
    number = int(input('Positive numbers less than 1000 only: '))
```

Note that this code also does not validate for non-numeric entry, which would have to be validated first.

168

Task 3

(The flowchart and pseudocode are the same as in Task 2.)

The following is an example of a GUI-based Python implementation:

Producing GUI
based applications
is outside the
syllabus.

```python
from tkinter import *

def validate_size():
    if int(entry_box.get()) < 0:
        error_label.config(text='Positive numbers only')
        entry_box.delete(0, END)
    elif int(entry_box.get()) > 1000:
        error_label.config(text='Must be less than 1000')
        entry_box.delete(0, END)
    else:
        # clear message label
        error_label.config(text='')

        # program continues as check is passed
    return int(entry_box.get())

# Create the main tkinter window
window = Tk()
window.title('My App')

# Add an empty tkinter label for error message
error_label = Label(window, width=25, height=1, text='')
error_label.grid(row=1, column=0)

# Add an entry box
entry_box = Entry(window, width=5)
entry_box.grid(row=0, column=0)

# Add a submit button
submit_button = Button(window, text='Submit Number', command=validate_size)
submit_button.grid(row=2, column=0)

# Enter the main event loop
window.mainloop()
```

Note how text input will crash the system. This would not be difficult to add to the same
function, which should then be renamed.

169

Task 4

a Figure 14.33 shows a flowchart and pseudocode for the algorithm.

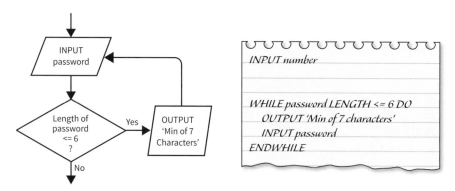

Figure 14.33 Flowchart and pseudocode for Task 4

b The following is an example of a text-based Python implementation:

```python
password = input('Insert password: ')

while len(password) <= 6:
    password = input('Insert password with a minimum of 7 characters: ')
```

Task 5

The following is an example of one possible solution for the function:

```python
def validate(num, pwd):
    if len(pwd) < 5:
        return False
    elif num < 1000 or num > 1500:
        return False
    else:
        return True
```

Task 6

Figure 14.34 shows a flowchart for `main()` and the `validate()` function.

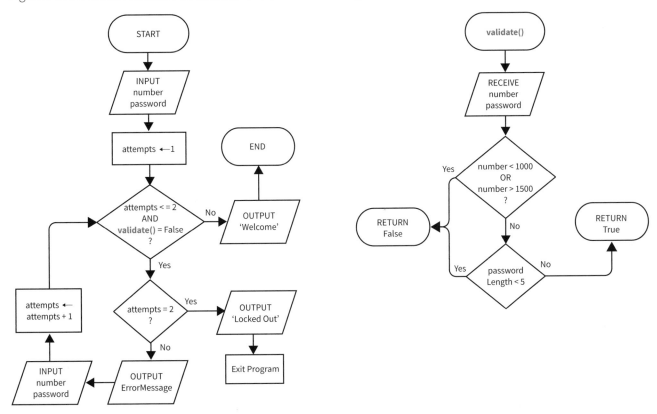

Figure 14.34 Flowchart solutions for Task 6

Here is the pseudocode for the main program:

```
INPUT number, password

attempts ← 1

WHILE validate(number, password)
= False AND attempts <=2 DO
    IF attempts = 2 THEN
        OUTPUT 'Locked Out'
        END Program
    ELSE
        OUTPUT 'Error'
        INPUT number, password
    ENDIF
ENDWHILE

OUTPUT 'Welcome'
```

The following is an example of a text-based Python implementation:

```python
import sys

# Validate function
def validate(num, pwd):
    if len(pwd) < 5:
        return False
    elif num < 1000 or num > 1500:
        return False
    else:
        return True

# Main program
number = int(input('Insert user number: '))
password = input('Insert your password: ')

attempts = 1
while validate(number, password) is False and attempts <= 2:
    if attempts == 2:
        print('Locked out')
        # Exit program
        sys.exit()
    else:
        print('Error')
        number = int(input('Insert user number between 1000 and 1500: '))
        password = input('Insert a password with at least 5 characters: ')

        # update attempts counter
        attempts = attempts + 1

if validate(number, password) == True:
    print('Welcome')
```

Chapter 10 – Testing

Task 1 – Trace Table Extension

x	y	w	Output	Comments
0	0	0		Initialisation values of the variables.
60	15	0		The new values are input.
45	15	1		x is reduced by 15, w is incremented by 1.
				Loop returns to the WHILE condition check. As x > y, loop runs.
30	15	2		x is reduced by 15, w is incremented by 1.
				Loop returns to the WHILE condition check. As x > y, loop runs.
15	15	3		x is reduced by 15, w is incremented by 1.
				Loop returns to the WHILE condition check. As x = y, loop exits.
			3	The value in w is output.

The output is incorrect as 60 quotient 15 = 4. The error is in the last iteration – the loop condition should read WHILE x >= y.

Task 2 – Discussion Question

a The aim of the flowchart is to return a^5. Use of trace tables with different input values can help to determine the purpose of unfamiliar programs.

b The flowchart is following the structure of a REPEAT . . . UNTIL loop.

Task 3 –Breakpoint

a The value passed to tins is correctly cast to an Integer as you cannot have a fraction of a tin of paint. The system makes use of simple division to calculate the number of tins of paint required; the resultant number is then rounded to an Integer. In some of your test cases, you should have found that this results in the number of tins being rounded down. In test cases where rounding area / coverage produces results with the decimal part of the answer being 0.5 or more, this is not a problem. Rounding down, though, will result in not having enough paint to complete the job.

b To resolve the problem, the number of tins calculated needs to be rounded up. This could be achieved in pseudocode by using a ROUND UP command. In Python this could be solved by importing the `math` library and using the `ceil()` function:

```
>>> 4.9*0.5
2.45
>>> int(4.9*0.5)
2
>>> import math
>>> math.ceil(4.9*0.5)
3
```

Task 4 – Beta testing

a Mobile phone numbers are pseudo-numbers with leading zeros so must be stored and handled as Strings. Age next birthday should be an Integer.

b and **c** Phone numbers:

Validation	Invalid data	Boundary data
Length Entry must be 12 characters long	07736 123456789 (over length) 07736 123 (under length)	Entries of 11, 12 and 13 characters
Format check The system stipulates the format: NNNNN–NNNNNN	077–36123456 07736 123456 077361–23456 +44 7736–123456	Not relevant
Type check Must only contain digits	07736–ABCDEF	Not relevant
Presence check	Null input – leave the input blank	Not relevant

Note that a range check would not be appropriate as the data is not of a true numeric format.

b and **c** Next birthday:

Validation	Invalid data	Boundary data
Type check Data must be an Integer	16.75 (must be whole number) Ten (must be a numeric value)	Not relevant
Range check The range should have reasonable minimum and maximum levels. The youngest patient could be newly born with an Age Next Birthday of 1. The other extreme could be set based on the maximum life expectancy; 110 would be reasonable.	–34 and 200 (Values well outside the expected boundaries)	0 and 1 (lower boundary) 109, 110 and 111 (upper boundary)
Presence check	Null input – leave the input blank	Not relevant

Task 5

a Input x = 16 and y = 7

x	y	w	Output	Comments
16	7	7		x and y are inputs, w = y
9	7	14		x = x – y, w = w + y, y unchanged Loops as x > 0
2	7	21		x = x – y, w = w + y, y unchanged Loops as x > 0
–5	7	28		x = x – y, w = w + y, y unchanged Loop ends as x < 0
			28	Value in w output

b Input x = 10 and y = 5

x	y	w	Output	Comments
10	5	5		x and y are inputs, w = y
5	5	10		x = x – y, w = w + w, y unchanged Loops as x > 0
0	5	15		x = x – y, w = w + y, y unchanged Loops as x = 0 (criteria in decision is x < 0)
–5	5	20		x = x – y, w = w + w, y unchanged Loop ends as x < 0
			20	Value in w output

This is a typical examination-style question that has been set to test your understanding of the difference between < and <= in the decision criteria.

Task 6

Error	Problem	Solution
factorial ← 1	The local declaration of the variable will result in its value being reset to 1 at every iteration of the loop.	Declare factorial as a global variable outside the loop.
FOR counter = 0 to number	Starting the iteration from zero will mean that `factorial` will be set to zero at the first iteration. From that point onwards as factorial is a multiple of itself the resultant multiplication will always be zero.	Set the iteration to run from 1: *FOR counter = 1 to number*
counter ← counter + 1	In a FOR loop, NEXT automatically increments the `counter` variable. As a result the loop will iterate with the value of counter being incremented by 2 on each iteration.	Remove this line of code.

Task 7

Error	Problem	Solution
small ← 0	Initialising the variable to zero will mean that `small` is always less than the value of any number input. As a result it will not record the lowest number.	**1** Initialise Small with a large value: *small ← 100000* **2** Set Small to the first Number input: *INPUT number* *small ← number* *WHILE number > 0*
WHILE number > 0	The input sequence should end when a negative number is input. The condition will end the loop when the user inputs a zero. Zero is not a negative number.	*WHILE number >= 0*
INPUT number	There is no input of `number` within the loop. As a result the value of `number` will only ever be the first value input and the algorithm will be an infinite loop.	Accept the input of number within the loop. It would be effective to add the line just before the LOOP terminator.

number ← small	Although the IF statement correctly checks the value of `number` against the value of `small` the action taken if `number` is less than `small` is incorrect. The assignment is the wrong way round – if the value of `small` is assigned to `number`, the lowest number would not be recorded and the incorrect value for `number` would be used in the remaining code.	Change the assignment statement:
		
		IF number < small THEN
		    small ← number
		ENDIF

OUTPUT sum	The output instruction is contained within the loop so the value of `sum` will be output every iteration. Although the final value output will accurately represented the sum of all the numbers input, the algorithm was intended to output the final sum value only, after the input sequence had ended.	Move this line out of the loop.

After making all those changes the corrected algorithm would look as follows:

```
sum ← 0

INPUT number
small ← number

WHILE number >= 0 DO
    IF number < small THEN
        small ← number
    ENDIF
    sum ← sum + number
    INPUT number
ENDWHILE

OUTPUT sum
OUTPUT small
```

Task 8

Height in metres is likely to be a fractional value so the most appropriate type is Real or Float.

Validation	Invalid data	Boundary data
Type check Data must be numeric	Two (must be a numeric value)	Not relevant
Range check The range should have reasonable minimum and maximum levels. The smallest height would be fairly low but not zero – a value of 0.5 could be reasonable. The other extreme could be set based on the maximum height of an adult – 2.6 metres would be reasonable. Other reasonable values are acceptable.	0.05 and 6 (values well outside the expected boundaries)	0.49, 0.5 and 0.51 (lower boundary) 2.59, 2.60 and 2.61 (upper boundary)
Presence check	Null input – leave the input blank	Not relevant

ID is a five-digit number. This might suggest an Integer but the scenario description does not exclude leading zeroes (00123 could be a valid ID) so the most appropriate type is String.

Validation	Invalid data	Boundary data
Type check Data must be numeric	1234A (must be a numeric value)	Not relevant
Length check Data must be five characters long	1234567 1234	Data of four, five and six characters
Presence check	Null input – leave the input blank	Not relevant

Surname is made up of alphanumeric characters so the most appropriate type is String.

Validation	Invalid data	Boundary data
Length check Any reasonable maximum length. Possibly 30 characters	Any data value of more than 30 characters	Data of 29, 30 and 31 characters
Presence check	Null input – leave the input blank	Not relevant

Chapter 11 – Arrays

Task 1

Appropriate validation approaches would include:

- provide range checks that limit the values of the two local variables called **index** (found in both functions) to the range 0 to 3.

- provide a type check which limits the user input entered in **tbox1**, **tbox2** and **tbox3** to Integer values.

Task 2

Figure 14.35(a) shows the flowchart for the input validation, using decisions and looping to pass execution back to accepting input if invalid data is entered. Figure 14.35(b) shows the flowchart for the output validation. Figure 14.36 shows the corresponding pseudocode for the processes.

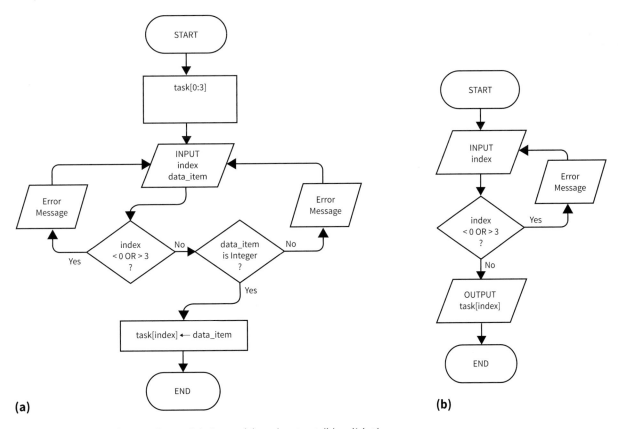

(a)   **(b)**

Figure 14.35 Flowcharts of possible input (a) and output (b) validation

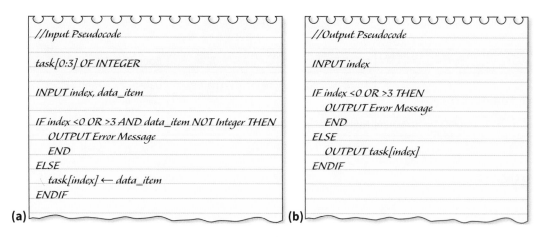

(a) (b)

Figure 14.36 Pseudocode of possible input (a) and output (b) validation

Task 3

The following code shows how the two functions could be amended. To provide a place for error messages, empty labels have been added to the GUI code (not shown). A full implementation can be found in the answers, which can be downloaded from the companion website at <u>cambridge.org/9781316617823</u>.

> Producing GUI based applications is outside the syllabus.

```python
# Functions
def input_data():
    # Clear any error message boxes
    label1.config(text='')
    label2.config(text='')
    label3.config(text='')

    # Validation of user input
    if int(tbox2.get()) < 0 or int(tbox2.get()) > 3:
        # clear text box and display message
        tbox2.delete(0, END)
        label2.config(text='Integer between 0 and 3 only')
        return
    else:
        index = int(tbox2.get())

    while True:
        try:
            data_item = int(tbox1.get())
            break
        except:
            # clear text box and display message
            tbox1.delete(0, END)
            label1.config(text='Integer only')
            return

    # insert new value into array
    task[index] = data_item
```

```
def output_data():
    # Clear any error message boxes
    label1.config(text='')
    label2.config(text='')
    label3.config(text='')

    # Validation of user input
    if int(tbox3.get()) < 0 or int(tbox3.get()) > 3:
        # clear text box and display message
        tbox3.delete(0, END)
        label3.config(text='Integer between 0 and 3 only')
        return
    else:
        index = int(tbox3.get())

    # clear output text box and display value
    tbox4.delete(0, END)
    tbox4.insert(END, task[index])
```

Note the use of **break** to escape from the **while True** loop and **return** to escape from the function.

Task 4

Figure 14.37 shows a flowchart and pseudocode for the algorithm.

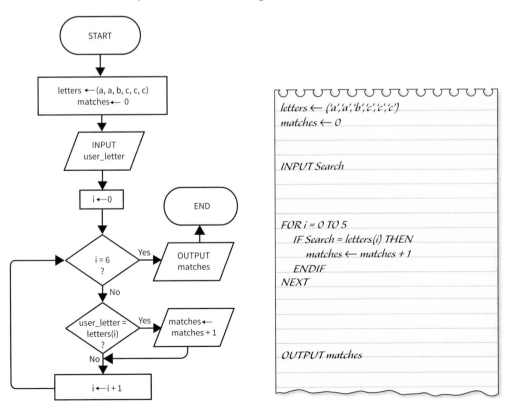

Figure 14.37 Flowchart and pseudocode for Task 4

Task 5

The following code is a possible solution:

```python
def search():

    letters = ['a','a','b','c','c','c']
    matches = 0
    user_letter = input('Enter the character to search for: ')

    # Perform search of letters
    for i in range(0,6):
        if user_letter == letters[i]:
            matches = matches + 1

    return matches


# Call function
number = search()

if number > 0:
    print('Your letter has been found', number, 'times.')
else:
    print('No match.')
```

Task 6

a Figure 14.38 shows a flowchart and pseudocode for the algorithm.

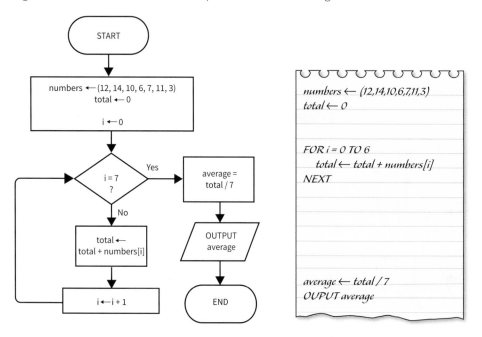

Figure 14.38 Flowchart and pseudocode for Task 6

b The following is an example implementation:

```
numbers = [12, 14, 10, 6, 7, 11, 3]
total = 0

for i in range(0,7):
    total = total + numbers[i]

average = total / 7

print(average)
```

Task 7

a Figure 14.39 shows a flowchart for the algorithms.

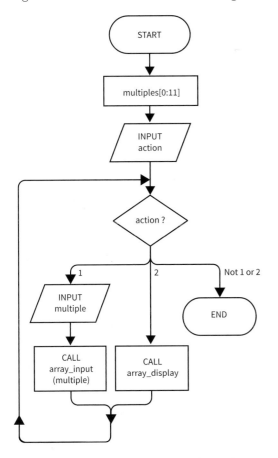
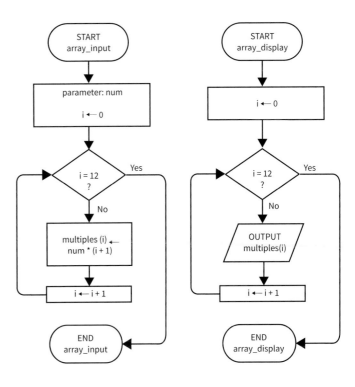

Figure 14.39 Flowchart solutions for Task 7

Figure 14.40 shows the pseudocode for a possible implementation.

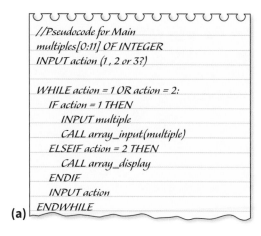

(a)

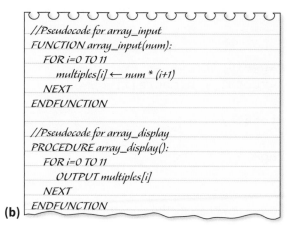

(b)

Figure 14.40 Pseudocode solutions for Task 7

b The following is an example implementation:

```
## Functions
def array_input(num):
    for i in range(0,12):
        multiples[i] = num * (i+1)

def array_display():
    for i in range(0,12):
        print(multiples[i])

## Main
# Declare an array with spaces for 12 data items
# Python equivalent of multiples[0:11] OF INTEGER
multiples = [None]*12

# Use triple quotes to make menu formatting easy
action = input('''Choose from:

1.Input
2.Display
3.Exit

[1, 2 or 3]? ''')

# Use a WHILE loop to allow the user to keep taking actions
# until Exit is chosen.
while action == '1' or action == '2':
    if action == '1':
        multiple = int(input('Input a whole number: '))
        array_input(multiple)
    elif action == '2':
        array_display()
    else:
        break
    action = int(input('\nChoose [1, 2 or 3]? '))
```

Task 8

a Figure 14.41 shows a flowchart and pseudocode for the algorithm.

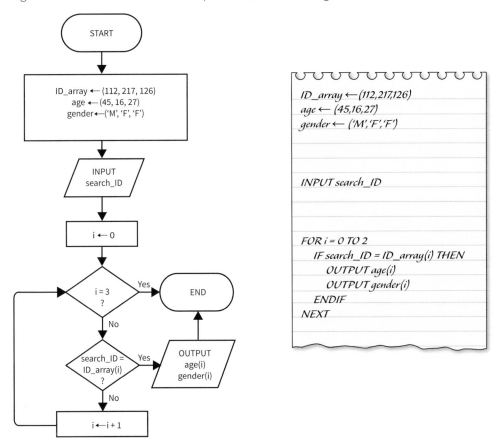

Figure 14.41 Flowchart and pseudocode for Task 8

b The following is an example Python implementation:

```python
# Initialise variables
ID_array = [112, 217, 126]
age = [45, 16, 27]
gender = ['M','F', 'F']

search_ID = int(input('Insert ID to Search: '))

for i in range(0,3):
    # Look for matching ID, if found print
    # out corresponding age and gender
    if search_ID == ID_array[i]:
        print('Age:', age[i])
        print('Gender:', gender[i])
```

Chapter 12 – Pre-release Task Preparation

Task 1

One possible first attempt at a Python implementation of TASK 1 is given below. Note, it is a good start but will not pass a strict testing regime. At the end of the script the arrays are printed out just so that we can see the process has taken place successfully.

```python
# task1.py

# Initialise the empty "arrays":
names = [None]*30
squad_shots = [None]*30
squad_assists = [None]*30
squad_goals = [None]*30
success_index = [None]*30

#### Main Loop
for i in range(3):
    # input name as a string
    name = input("Enter player's name: ")
    names[i] = name

    # input and validate numerical data (first attempt)
    while True:
        shots = int(input("Enter shots made: "))
        if shots > 100 or shots < 0:
            print("Error: Unexpected input")
        else:
            break

    while True:
        assists = int(input("Enter assists made: "))
        if assists > 50 or assists < 0:
            print("Error: Unexpected input")
        else:
            break

    while True:
        goals = int(input("Enter goals scored: "))
        if goals > 40 or goals < 0:
            print("Error: Unexpected input")
        else:
            break

    # load the "arrays"
    squad_shots[i] = shots
    squad_assists[i] = assists
    squad_goals[i] = goals
```

```
# Print "arrays"
print(names)
print(squad_shots)
print(squad_assists)
print(squad_goals)
```

Task 2

One possible first attempt at a Python implementation of TASK 1 and 2 is given below:

```
# task2.py

# Initialise the empty "arrays":
names = [None]*30
squad_shots = [None]*30
squad_assists = [None]*30
squad_goals = [None]*30
success_index = [None]*30

# Initialise global variables
squad_total = 0

#### Main Loop
for i in range(3):
    # input name as a string
    name = input("Enter player's name: ")
    names[i] = name

    # input and validate numerical data (first attempt)
    while True:
        shots = int(input("Enter shots made: "))
        if shots > 100 or shots < 0:
            print("Error: Unexpected input")
        else:
            break

    while True:
        assists = int(input("Enter assists made: "))
        if assists > 50 or assists < 0:
            print("Error: Unexpected input")
        else:
            break

    while True:
        goals = int(input("Enter goals scored: "))
        if goals > 40 or goals < 0:
            print("Error: Unexpected input")
        else:
            break
```

```
    # load the "arrays"
    squad_shots[i] = shots
    squad_assists[i] = assists
    squad_goals[i] = goals

    # process scores
    success_index[i] = assists + (2*shots) + (3*goals)
    squad_total = squad_total + success_index[i]

    # print current players' success index
    print(name, success_index[i])

# Calculate squad average
squad_average = squad_total / 3

# Print final summary
print("\nSquad average:", squad_average)
```

Task 3
One possible first attempt at a Python implementation of TASK 1, 2 and 3 is given
below:
```
# task3.py

# Initialise the empty "arrays":
names = [None]*30
squad_shots = [None]*30
squad_assists = [None]*30
squad_goals = [None]*30
success_index = [None]*30

# Initialise global variables
squad_total = 0
success_highest = 0
player_highest = ""

#### Main Loop
for i in range(3):
    # input name as a string
    name = input("Enter player's name: ")
    names[i] = name

    # input and validate numerical data (first attempt)
    while True:
        shots = int(input("Enter shots made: "))
        if shots > 100 or shots < 0:
            print("Error: Unexpected input")
        else:
            break
```

```
    while True:
        assists = int(input("Enter assists made: "))
        if assists > 50 or assists < 0:
            print("Error: Unexpected input")
        else:
            break
    while True:
        goals = int(input("Enter goals scored: "))
        if goals > 40 or goals < 0:
            print("Error: Unexpected input")
        else:
            break

    # load the "arrays"
    squad_shots[i] = shots
    squad_assists[i] = assists
    squad_goals[i] = goals

    # process scores
    success_index[i] = assists + (2*shots) + (3*goals)
    squad_total = squad_total + success_index[i]

    # print current player's success_index
    print(name, success_index[i])

    # keep track of highest scoring player
    if success_index[i] > success_highest:
        success_highest = success_index[i]
        player_highest = name

# Calculate squad average
squad_average = sqaud_total / 3

# Print final summary
print("Squad average:", squad_average)
print("Most successful player:", player_highest, "with", success_highest)
```

Task 4 – Test Data

The test data needs to include:

<u>normal data</u> such as 76, 45, and 12

<u>non-integers</u> such as 13.5 and a string such as fred (both of which should be handled by error messages and the user should be asked for new input)

<u>out of range data</u> such as -1, 102, 51 and 42 (which should be accepted handled by error messages and the user should be asked for new input)

<u>limit scores</u> such as 100, 50, 40 and 0 (which should all be accepted and handled correctly)

Chapter 13 – Examination Practice

Mark schemes for examination-style questions. These mark schemes have been written by the author. In examination, the way marks are awarded to answers like these may be different.

Question 1

Size	Country	Output
20	USA	10
19	France	19
14	UK	16

(1 mark)

(1 mark)

(1 mark)

Question 2

Error	Effect	Correction	
Small has been initialised to zero	Small is likely to be smaller than any of the array values and will not be changed by the comparison with the number input.	Either of following would be acceptable: Initialise Small with a large number. OR Assign the value of Num(1) to Small before any comparison is made with the remaining array values.	(1 mark for error) (1 mark for correction)
Num(Counter) ← Small	The value of Small is placed into the array.	Small ← Num(Counter)	(1 mark for error) (1 mark for correction)
The loop counter is incremented twice	Next automatically increments the loop but the following line also increments the loop counter: Counter ← Counter + 1 Consequently only the odd number indexes will be read.	Remove the line Counter ← Counter + 1	(1 mark for error) (1 mark for correction)
Small is output from within the FOR loop	The system will output the current value of Small on every iteration.	Put the OUTPUT line after NEXT.	(1 mark for error) (1 mark for correction)

Question 3

Time	Total	Number	Count	Average	Output
	0	0	0		
18	18	0	1		
19	37	0	2		
24	61	1	3		
21	82	2	4		
18	100	2	5		
17	117	2	6		
23	140	3	7		
20	160	4	8		
19	179	4	9		
21	200	5	10		
−1	200	5	10	20	
					20, 5
(1 mark)	(1 mark)	(1 mark)	(1 mark)	(1 mark)	(1 mark)

It is likely that mistakes would not be penalised twice. As a result, if the Total, Number or Count are incorrect the marks will be lost in those columns. However, if those incorrect values have been used to produce the Average and Output then the marks for those columns may well remain.

The Total, Number, Count columns must start with a zero – the algorithm initialised these variables and this should be included in the trace table. The Average and Output columns must not contain values (not even zero) during the execution of the loop. They are outside the loop in the algorithm and do not take a value before the input of the final –1.

Question 4

Any effective algorithm will gain marks; this is an example:

```
INPUT N1, N2, N3
IF N1 < N2 AND N1 < N3 THEN
    OUTPUT N1
ELSEIF N2 < N3 THEN
    OUTPUT N2
ELSE
    OUTPUT N3
ENDIF
```

Correct method to find smallest where N1 is smallest.					(1 mark)

Correct method to find smallest where N2 is smallest.					(1 mark)

Correct method to find smallest where N3 is smallest.					(1 mark)

Question 5

Data input	Validation technique	Invalid test data
Mobile phone number	**Length check:** 10 or 11 characters	Any invalid data, e.g. 07716 123 or 07736 123456789
	Format check: NNNNN–NNNNNN	ABCDE_123456
Height of a person	**Type check:** Real (not Integer; Height will not be only whole numbers)	Any invalid data, e.g. 2½ or 'Ninety centimetres'
	Range check: 0.25 to 3 metres (accept other sensible ranges)	4.6 metres, 1 cm
Number of brothers	**Type check:** Integer (must be a whole number, so not Real or Short)	4.3, Four
	Range check: 0 to 20 (any sensible large value)	–2, not zero – you can have no brothers

For each of the data items:

Correct validation method.					(1 mark)

Appropriate test data – must match the validation method stated.					(1 mark)

(Total of 6 marks)

Question 6

Number	Count	Output
11	0	
8	1	
5	2	
2	3	
–1	4	4
9	0	
6	1	
3	2	
0	3	
–3	4	4
–2		End of sequence

1 mark for each correct section as indicated above.

Output must not contain any additional items.

(Total of 4 marks)

Question 7

```
PENDOWN
RIGHT 90
REPEAT 3
```

```
        FORWARD 30
        RIGHT 90
    ENDREPEAT
```

```
    FORWARD 10
    LEFT  90
    FORWARD 30
    PEN UP
```

```
    FORWARD 10
    PENDOWN
    FORWARD 10
    RIGHT 90
```

```
    FORWARD 20
    RIGHT 90
    FORWARD 30
```

1 mark for each correct section as indicated.

(Total of 4 marks)

Question 8

1 mark for each correctly completed section as indicated in Figure 14.42.

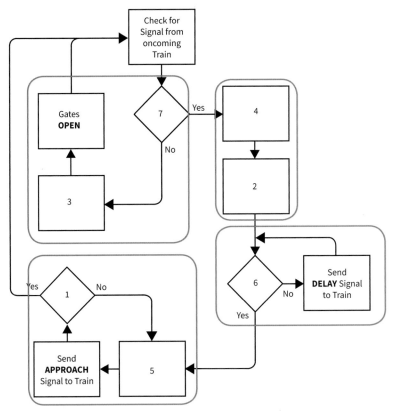

Figure 14.42 Flowchart solution for Question 8

Question 9

Any effective algorithm will gain marks; this is an example:

```
INPUT TargetScore
FOR Counter = 1 TO 6
    IF Score(Counter) > TargetScore THEN
        OUTPUT Name(Counter)
        OUTPUT ID(Counter)
    ENDIF
NEXT
```

Correct loop to iterate six times.	(1 mark)
Correct comparison for TargetScore	(1 mark)
Correct output of Name and ID within loop	(1 mark)

Question 10

Any effective algorithm will gain marks; Figure 14.43 gives examples:

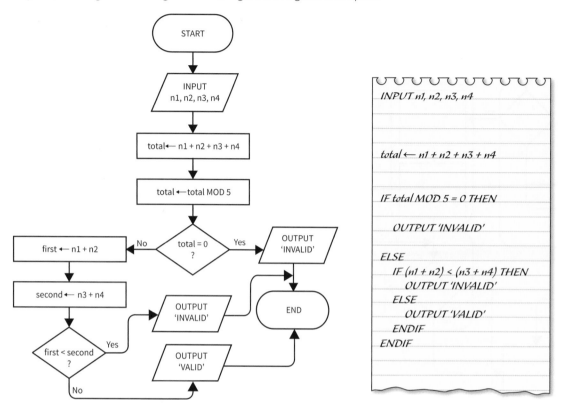

Figure 14.43 Flowchart and pseudocode solutions for Question 10

No need to use total, first and second as shown in the example. (This could be achieved in a single step.)

Correct calculation of total.	(1 mark)
Correct check that not a multiple of 5.	(1 mark)
Correct calculation of first and second.	(1 mark)
Correct comparison of first and second.	(1 mark)
Correct output of 'INVALID' from both paths.	(1 mark)
Correct output of 'VALID'.	(1 mark)
	(Total of 6 marks)

Appendix: Tkinter Reference

This appendix is intended as a quick reminder of the code required to add tkinter widgets to your GUIs. It is not a Cambridge IGCSE and O Level Computer Science syllabus requirement to build GUI applications. However, it is also not very difficult to do.

Producing GUI based applications is outside the syllabus.

An Empty Window

```
from tkinter import *

# Create the main tkinter window
window = Tk()
window.title('My Application')

# Add widgets here

# Enter the main event loop
window.mainloop()
```

A Frame

```
frame1 = Frame(window,height=20, width=100, bg='green')
frame1.grid(row=0, column=0)
```

A Label

```
my_label = Label(window, width=25, height=1, text='My Label')
my_label.grid(row=0, column=0)
```

An Image Label

```
# Import gif image from images folder in the same folder as the script
my_image = PhotoImage(file='images/my_image.gif')

# Add image to label widget
my_label = Label(window, image='my_image')
my_label.grid(row=0, column=0)
```

An Empty Label as a Spacer

```
my_label = Label(window, width=20, height=1, text='')
my_label.grid(row=0, column=0)
```

A Button

```
my_button = Button(window, text='Submit', width=10, command=click_function)
my_button.grid(row=1, column=0)
```

A Text Entry Box

```
my_text_box = Entry(window, width=15)
my_text_box.grid(row=0, column=0)
```

A Text Box

```
my_text_box = Text(window, width=15, height=5)
my_text_box.grid(row=0, column=0)
```

A Scrolling Text Box

```
my_text_box = ScrolledText(window, width=15, height=5, wrap=WORD)
my_text_box.grid(row=0, column=0)
```

A Drop-down Menu (with Integers)

```
# Create a tuple of menu items
options = (1,2,3)

# Create a tkinter string variable object for the radiobuttons
my_variable_object = IntVar() # access the value with my_variable_object.get()
my_variable_object.set('choose:')
my_dropdown = OptionMenu(window, my_variable_object, *options)
my_dropdown.grid(row=0, column=0)
```

Radio Button Menu (with Strings)

```
# Create a tkinter string variable object for the radiobuttons
gender = StringVar() # access the value with my_variable.get()

# Add two radiobutton widgets
radio1 = Radiobutton(window, text='Female', variable=gender, value='female')
radio1.grid(row=0, column=0)
radio1.select() # pre-selects this radio button
radio2 = Radiobutton(window, text='Male', variable=gender, value='male')
radio2.grid(row=1, column=0)
```

Checkboxes

```
# Create three checkboxes
# var1, var2 and var3 return either 0 (unselected) or 1 (selected)
var1 = IntVar() # access the value with var1.get()
checkbox1 = Checkbutton(window, text='Python', variable=var1)
checkbox1.grid(row=0, column=0)

var2 = IntVar() # access the value with var2.get()
checkbox2 = Checkbutton(window, text='Visual Basic', variable=var2)
checkbox2.grid(row=1, column=0)

var3 = IntVar() # access the value with var3.get()
checkbox3 = Checkbutton(window, text='Java', variable=var3)
checkbox3.grid(row=2, column=0)
```